The Big Uglies

*Transitioning from the Glory Days
To a Life of Glory*

By: Bob Brenner with Reji Laberje

Readers talk about Bob's first book,

"Live An Extreme Life"

"Five Stars! What an inspirational book."

~Renee McCarthy

"Great read. Life changing book."

~Jeffrey L Machton

"I would highly recommend it as something to help inspire you . . . This isn't a diet book. It is one man's story of how weight loss was one of his many demons he had to deal with. It is inspirational. I would highly recommend it as something to help inspire you . . . with the help of God and others!"

~Marilyn Corby

"Don't miss this one! Such an inspirational story of one man's fall into addiction and his climb out of the dark hole that almost broke his family,

destroyed his spirit and potentially could have brought about the end of his life. Reality television is only able to show you a glimpse into a person's life, and this book filled in many pieces of Bob Brenner's transformation. One cannot help but admire the depth of his honesty, as Bob shares the dark side of his personality, and his addiction-riddled past. (I) will re-read many passages again and again when I am lagging in motivation during my own transformational journey."

~Shauna Head

Scan here to purchase
"Live An Extreme Life"
http://www.amazon.com/Live-Extreme-Life-Gaining-Purpose/dp/0989309584/ref=asap_bc?ie=UTF8

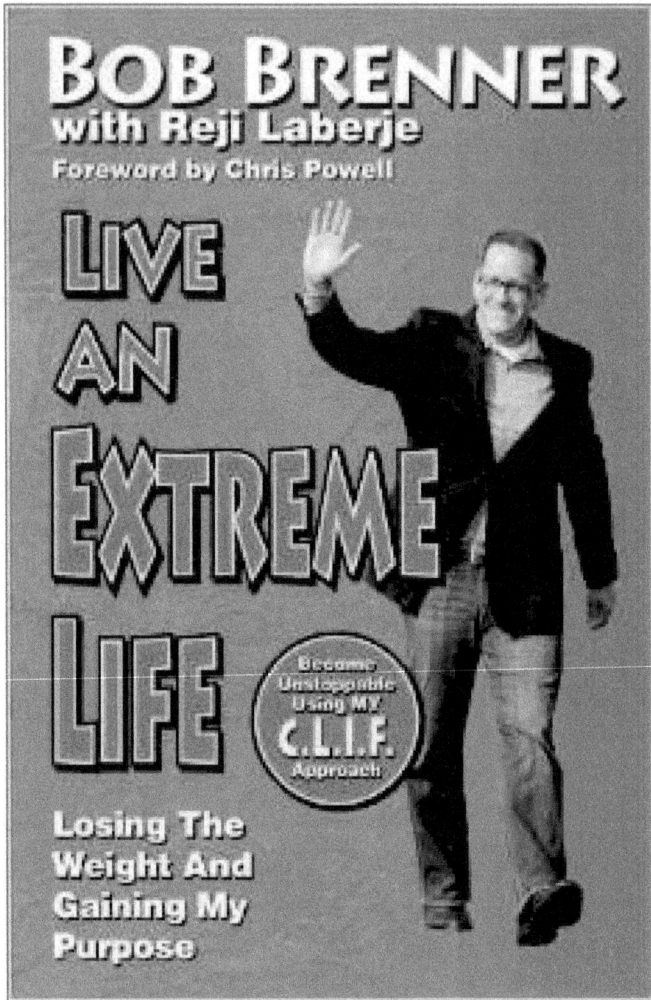

Bob Brenner's first book,
"Live An Extreme Life."
Available everywhere fine books are sold.

This work is based on the experiences of an individual. Every effort has been made to ensure the accuracy of the content.

Quantity order requests can be emailed to:
publishing@rejilaberje.com
Or mailed to: Reji Laberje Author Programs, Publishing Orders, 234 W. Broadway Street, Waukesha, WI 53186

Brenner, Bob
The Big Uglies

Contributing Author: RejiLaberje, RejiLaberjeAuthorPrograms
Contributing Editor: Michael Nicloy
Interior Design: Reji Laberje
Cover Design: Michael Nicloy
Photos: Bob Brenner, Andy Drefs, Kimberly Laberge, Chris McIntosh, Vince Papale, Bruce Pitcher, Dr. Holly Wyatt, Barb Brenner

ISBN-10: 0692649379
ISBN-13:978-0692649374
BISAC Codes:
OCC019000 BODY, MIND & SPIRIT / Inspiration & Personal Growth
HEA010000 HEALTH& FITNESS / Healthy Living
BIO026000 BIOGRAPHY & AUTOBIOGRAPHY / Personal Memoirs

Author Programs, LLC.

www.rejilaberje.com

"The Big Uglies" doesn't happen without the incredible people that God has put into my life.

"For I know the plans I have for you, says the lord. They are plans for good and not for disaster, to give you a future and a hope."

~Jeremiah 29:11

I dedicate this book to my incredible wife, Kelly, my children, Kayla and Jordan, my parents, brothers and sister, coaches, mentors, and friends. You all have impacted my life more than you know and I'm a truly blessed man!

I love you all!

~Bob

Table Of Contents

Forward

We played for him and we played for one another.

Life happens; what are you gonna do about it?

LIVE BIG – NOT UGLY!

> *Bruce Pitcher Ignites The Day!*

My Big Uglies had me living a LIE

> *L.iving Large: Selfishness*

> *Life of I.mbalance: Pride*

> *Sense of E.ntitlement: Ego*

LIVE BIG – NOT UGLY!

> *Vince Papale's Invincible Moments!*

The field changed.

LIVE BIG – NOT UGLY!

> *Dr. Holly's Mental Mindset!*

Read the play in front of you

LIVE BIG – NOT UGLY!

> *Chris McIntosh's Five Seconds!*

My big life is not about me.

Resources

Index of QR Codes

Index of Photos

Acknowledgments

About the Authors

"The Big Uglies" is Bob Brenner's second book since he lost 253 pounds in a single year with the help of Chris and Heidi Powell of ABC's *"Extreme Weight Loss."* His first book, *"Live an Extreme Life: Losing the Weight and Gaining My Purpose,"* chronicles not only his journey from 448 lbs. to 195 lbs., but also his journey from a hopeless man to one who would *bring* hope to millions of people around the world.

> *"An extremely inspirational (story). This guy has a back story I am not sure I could have recovered from. I am so glad he put his story on paper to give the rest of us hope for a brighter future!"*
>
> *~D. Bailey*

Sadly, not everybody who makes a physical transformation in a short period of time manages to maintain the weight loss. In fact, according to livestrong.com, only 5% of people who lose weight quickly (such as through a crash diet) will keep that weight off. Bob took his transformation beyond the physical, though. He has kept up his physical transformation because he succeeded in attaining a transformed heart, mind, and spirit.

Bob signs copies of his book at its September, 2014 book release.

Since the release of *"Live An Extreme Life,"* Bob retired from his long career with the Waukesha (Wisconsin) Sheriff's Department where he served as everything from jailer, to detective, to a respected leader as a narcotics officer working with local, state, and federal agencies.

(At Bob's 2015 retirement ceremony, Waukesha County Sheriff, Eric Severson, thanks Bob for his years of service and dedication.)

With his policing days behind him, but his heart of service still strong, Bob was able to focus on the life that had come to him as a motivational speaker, life coach, and transformation specialist. Bob has spoken to tens of thousands across the United States since 2013, helping to change lives and hearts everywhere he goes.

He realized in his travels that there were many people like him, former athletes and coaches who had left the games with all of the Big Ugly habits of the sports they loved, while simultaneously forgetting the lessons of success that came from those games. Going through what he'd been through: being an athlete, coaching athletes, and living unhealthy for more than twenty years following that athleticism, he was able to recognize so many people like himself who just didn't know where to go when the clock ticked down at the end of the last game. Bob realized that when a person is done being an athlete, that doesn't mean he or she has to be done living as an athlete in life. The field changes. There are ways to tackle new challenges by using the positives that come from the games and leaving behind the negatives.

Because of Bob's success in personal and physical transformation, a success that he has maintained for years since his 56% weight loss, he has been blessed with an opportunity to reach others and he wants to teach them what it takes to live BIG, like they did when they were athletes, without living UGLY, as he had done for twenty years. It is that "next field" in life that Bob addresses in his next chapter . . .

"The Big Uglies" is a Reji Laberje Author Programs interactive text. Throughout the book, you will find QR codes that will provide a little more insight into what is being shared. Find a free QR scanner for your smart device via a search through your device's app store. Then, you can scan the QR code with your smart device to discover the online resources. In addition, all of the information from the QR codes can be found on the Electronic Resource Hub (ERH) for *"The Big Uglies."*

Want to try it out? Visit the ERH through the below QR code and good luck living BIG . . . but not UGLY!

Electronic Resource Hub
"The Big Uglies"
www.rejilaberje.com/bob-brenner.html

TheBig

Uglies

In American Football, a lineman is a player who specializes in play at the line of scrimmage. The linemen on the team currently in possession of the ball are the offensive linemen.

You're at the line of scrimmage of your own life and you need to advance. Are you ready to get BIG in your life?

1

We played for him and we played for one another.

> *"No one wants to die. Even people who want to go to heaven don't want to die to get there. And yet death is the destination we all share. No one has ever escaped it. And that is as it should be, because Death is very likely the single best invention of Life. It is Life's change agent."*
>
> *~Steve Jobs*

It was my sophomore year of high school at Westosha Central High School in Paddock Lake, Wisconsin. I was pulled up to play on varsity, at my usual position as one of the offensive linemen. We had a team that wasn't expected to do much that year. Our program was failing. It was the year of Coach Ken Wagner's arrival.

"I don't care where you were before," he told us. "This season is about where you are, now."

On the line with me was a senior aptly named Jimmy. Like his name, Jimmy exemplified American boyhood. At linebacker and center, he was a phenomenal player. He was a straight-A student athlete who was ready to follow-up his successful high school career by going to the Air Force Academy. Jimmy lived just two doors down from me and he had been my neighbor for twelve years. He'd spent time with my family and was just an all-around good guy.

I don't know if it was in his nature or because I was in his neighborhood, but Jimmy was the guy who would always lift me up and be a good friend to me. My older brothers would pick on me, like big brothers are meant to do, and Jimmy would gently be there for me by just being a good friend. Everybody loved Jimmy whose only fault seemed to be a lead foot, as he had received a second speeding ticket that we'd all heard about. There are worse sins.

One afternoon, Jimmy wasn't at practice. We all thought it was kind of weird.

Jimmy had shot himself.

This tremendous student and athlete and friend and player and person had taken his own life. Nobody understood the reasons why, but do we ever?

Thursday night practice came and emotions were running high. We had a game the next day and this season was now going to be played for Jimmy. Football was easier to understand than life. It was a coping mechanism for something we couldn't fathom having to cope with at all.

On the field we understood, we would be allowed to:

SWEAT

   AND SCREAM

AND HIT

    AND GRUNT

     AND POUND OUR CHESTS

     AND RUN

AND SHAKE OUR FISTS AT THE SKY

AND PUNCH OUR KNUCKLES INTO THE GROUND.

We could do all the things a person wants to do when grieving, but can't because it's somehow not considered to be acceptable behavior. Then, if we did it right, we could come out winners in this losing situation.

We could do the next things we needed to do:

hug

and cry

and hold onto one another

and lift each other up.

Hell, a good game of football is a good session of therapy. It should be prescribed as a fast-forward button through the stages of grief.

Coach Ken Wagner, on Thursdays after practice, would take the team to go eat dinner, and then meet at a local church in silence where he would tell us to think about our next day—game day. It would be really controversial to do such a thing today, but—on that Thursday—it was needed. Losing Jimmy bonded us further and we dedicated that season to him. We would win it for Jimmy with unity.

Not only did Coach Wagner implement unity, but he implemented a belief system. He told us that we *could* do well. He expected excellence.

"You guys are a unit. As the offensive linemen, you are one. Since you are one, you will hold hands, fight together, be together, and lift one another up. You stand side-by-side together."

The coach introduced the practice of hand holding for the offensive linemen. The team would enter the field both side-by-side and hand-in-hand. Here was a group of the biggest guys in the school, walking out of the locker room linked together like parents and children. The hand-holding wasn't Wagner's original idea. The history of the practice by linemen is deep in college. It represents solidarity – something for which we desperately hungered. Still, to throw such a concept at high school boys was new and uncomfortable.

The first time coach had us grab onto the player next to us, it felt weird, to be honest. It didn't feel natural. It was a little too "touchy-feely" for me. But, I also remember being in a huddle when it was fourth and one and you'd reach over, grab a hand, and feel the guy next to you squeezing back as if to say, *'Yes! Let's do it!'* You could feel the intensity of the person next to you and absorb it. It was like an electric pulse through the huddle.

After Jimmy died, the linemen didn't even flinch grabbing the hands of the guys next to them. We stood in solidarity and I don't even remember who we played, anymore, but I do remember that we beat the hell out of them. We left all of our emotion on the field.

We took what life gave us . . . what *death* gave us; we went onto the field and we won. We took that negative and worked to turn it into a positive. That season we had the option of doing one of two things. We couldgive up or we could remember Jimmy as a friend and teammate and bust our tails on the rest of the season in his honor.

That season, when we weren't expected to accomplish much of anything, we only lost two games. Jimmy was still lifting us up. We played for him and we played for one another.

While the stakes may have been higher that season, playing for one another wasn't new to being a part of the offensive line. My understanding of solidarity in that community of offensive line brothers began when I was in elementary school and continued past high school into my college career, as well as the years I spent coaching my own son.

In the fifth grade, I became a part of the line under Coach John Hansen. There was a separation at that age between the skilled and non-skilled players. The linemen were the chubby, not good enough, not fast enough players. We were definitely, at times, considered almost like a lower class of player. We were certainly not the guys getting the glory. Nobody wanted to play on the offensive line.

We weren't running.

We weren't throwing.

We weren't even attacking, which was reserved for the defensive linemen; no sacks for us.

Offensive linemen are "just" blockers and we were—quite frankly, at that age—the *fat kids.* If you take a bunch of fat kids, throw them around on a dirty football field for a couple of hours where they will sweat and hit one another until they're black and blue, then they're no longer just big; they're ugly. We *were* the "BIG UGLIES."

- *According to his "The Michigan Daily,"Famous American Sportscaster, Keith Jackson (ABC Sports 1966-2006) often referred to offensive and defensive line players as the "Big Uglies."*

- *David Duda is a super fan of sorts for Penn State, ESPN reported in its "Big Ten Blog."(He) throws on (an) ugly mask and fires up the Penn State football crowd . . . everyone knows of the "Big Uglies" in Happy Valley.*

- *Sportswriter, Lisa Horne, may have said it best, though, when she wrote in the online blog, "Scout:" 'The "Big Uglies." They battle in the trenches to protect the quarterback or create holes for a running back. They're the heart of the offense and a critical component in moving the chains. Without an experienced offensive line, a great quarterback can look ordinary and a fast running back can get stuffed.'"*

I don't think it was really until high school that we had coaches who made the linemen feel special. From that point on, I did get the opportunity to work with a lot of coaches who used the linemen to make the team go. Without the linemen, the playmakers can't make the plays. Defensive linemen stop the other side from making the play. Offensive linemen stop the defensive linemen.

While coaches emphasized our role, we also got lucky in high school to have guys like my buddy, Rob Hall. He hung out with the linemen and he was a running back . . . a playmaker. Rob was the first guy that really showed appreciation for the linemen. We protected him and opened up holes for him to run in. He got it.

Being called a Big Ugly was never an insult. It was the identity of a protector. It was a guy who would lift up others who would get the glory, but the glory of a shared goal, nonetheless. There was nothing about being a Big Ugly that was actually ugly. On the contrary, we learned to approach every game with:

- *Unity*
- *Timing*
- *Intellect*

Unfortunately, the football game also left some scars that really were ugly. Living an athlete's life gave me:

- A *"L.ive Large" Life of Gluttony*
- A *Lifestyle of I.mbalance*
- A *Sense of E.ntitlement*

It would take years, decades really, before I ended the LIE and rediscovered the positive aspects of unity, timing, and intellect to help me live a life that was big . . . but not ugly.

Brenner's fellow Wisconsinite, Mike Webster, was a Center for the Pittsburgh Steelers from 1974 to 1990, during which time he was named Captain and helped his team take home four Super Bowl championships!

A strong force at your center can lead to a championship life.

2

Life happens; what are you gonna do about it?

"We cannot always control everything that happens to us in this life, but we can control how we respond. Many struggles come as problems and pressures that sometimes cause pain. Others come as temptations, trials, and tribulations.

~L. Lionel Kendrick

Despite playing the game since elementary school and a family that thought I could be the one who went pro one day, I didn't go to the college that had initially recruited me for my football skills. The coaching staff at the recruiting school had treated me like a king when I visited the campus, but—when at an unrelated visit to my high school—the head coach didn't even remember who I was. It was a huge shot to my ego. As a high school kid who thinks he could go places with football, it just kind of sucked. I chose to attend a local college and, at the same time, I watched my best friend, the man I'd protected on the line since the fifth grade, move away to Florida.

From there on out, adult life came calling. I was about to go from living big to living ugly, after a whirlwind journey I recollected in *"Live An Extreme Life:"*

Life put me on the fast track with school, and with family, so I also hopped on the fast track when it came to my police career.

- *In spring of 1991, I finished my semester of school majoring in Criminal Justice.*
- *I took off the next school year (fall of 1991 to spring of 1992).*
- *I got married to my wife, Kelly.*
- *I went back to school in fall of 1992, (really just to play football because I had two years of eligibility left on the team).*
- *I got a job in December of that year at the Waukesha County Jail.*
- *I had my daughter in February of 1993.*

- *I went back to school, again, now a married father of one, in fall of 1993.*

I had twenty-four credits to go, but I was married with a kid. My wife was making minimum wage. I was attempting full-time school, a full-time job, and overtime work just to be able to buy groceries and pay the bills . . . I couldn't do it all anymore! I decided it was time to jump into my career with both feet.

From football playing college kid, to full-time working family man; from the college campus to the county lockup . . . This was my new life. This was my new commitment, commitment to the job; commitment to financially take care of my family; commitment to provide for a kid . . . when I still felt like a kid, myself.

Life happens; what are you gonna do about it? **If you give me a room full of everybody whose life has turned out exactly the way he or she expected it to turn out, I'll give you an *empty room.*** Even those people who end up living their childhood dream jobs don't necessarily take the paths they plotted out as children.

When my life's field changed from the football field, I didn't change with it.

On the football field, nobody represented UNITY like my linemen and I. We were the most cohesive group out there! We practiced in groups. We sometimes literally carried one another. We did everything together as a team. We were an entourage everywhere we went.

On the field, we prided ourselves on being the smart, tempo-setters of the game. The quarterback can't throw if the linemen don't block. We were brothers and the rest of the team was, to us, our extended family – our cousins.

Off the football field, when we weren't in season, drinking parties were huge. There was a lot of peer pressure for those who didn't really want to join in. *'We do everything as a team!'* Participation in the over-the-top, high-caloric-content meals and the under-the-radar, high-alcoholic-content parties were an expectation.

Even in college, we would go out *as a group* – as an offensive line – our brotherhood. On road trips, usually at an after-game buffet, we'd eat together. Unity was our brand and, if you were a Big Ugly, you participated.

When I was no longer playing, I kept at the role of unifying social leader. I was the guy who could out-eat anyone and play the role of everybody's favorite drunk, leading my "teammates" as I got bigger and uglier.

On the football field, TIMING mattered and timing was control. Timing began with the huddle, holding hands and listening to the quarterback in front of us. When we broke the huddle, we would immediately set the tempo. If we hustled to the line, the rest of the team hustled. If we sauntered, so did our teammates.

Timing continued in our alignment. We would set the tempo for how fast the ball had to get off. We would read whether the play would have to move quickly or not. Usually, in football, it moves quickly. We controlled the people in front of us, by controlling our physicality, (at least, when we were doing our job right); that control would ultimately bring control to the whole game.

Off the football field, we set the social pace. On the road, or after practices, we would take in serious food and calories and take them in quickly. An Italian restaurant in town had "all you can eat pasta" and they hated seeing us coming. It was always a hurry-up offense when it came to playing at life. Everything was fast and extreme and, contrary to life on the field, the pace spun us out of control.

When I was no longer playing, I kept at the practice of setting the timing of my life, regardless of who else was in the picture. I tried to control people like I had done on the line, but my own life was out of control. I was eating myself to death, as I got bigger and uglier.

On the football field, INTELLECT was mandatory. Using intellect, as offensive linemen, we had to learn to read the different looks from our opponents, as well as their body language. We had to be able to adapt.

'Is there a blitz coming?'

'Are they moving from the outside to the inside or vice versa?'

We had to read the defense, know the play, know the snap count, and we had to know . . . *immediately*. The plays were physical and aggressive, but they were also intentional. Thought went into what had to come first, what required our attention, and what we needed to protect our brothers from.

Off the football field, when I was no longer playing, I kept the ego of intellectualism. I kept thinking I could read the world. I didn't need somebody to tell me what was going on around me. That was my job.

But . . .

I was failing at knowing priorities.

I was failing at protecting the people in my life.

I got bigger and uglier.

I had kept all sorts of Big Ugly habits from my football playing days, but none of the true UNITY, TIMING, and INTELLECT that I had learned and developed as one of the "Big Uglies."

More than twenty years after my football playing days were done, there was little left of the player I once was and so much more of the man I had become.

- I was selfish, food addicted, and alcoholic.
- My priorities had left loved ones emotionally abandoned.
- The only thing bigger than my stack of bills was my belt.
- I couldn't fit the bullet-proof vest I needed to protect my body during my police work.

- I didn't want to look at the body I couldn't protect in the mirror.
- In short, twenty-five years of a football-less football life left me a 448 pound bankrupt drunk with a broken marriage.

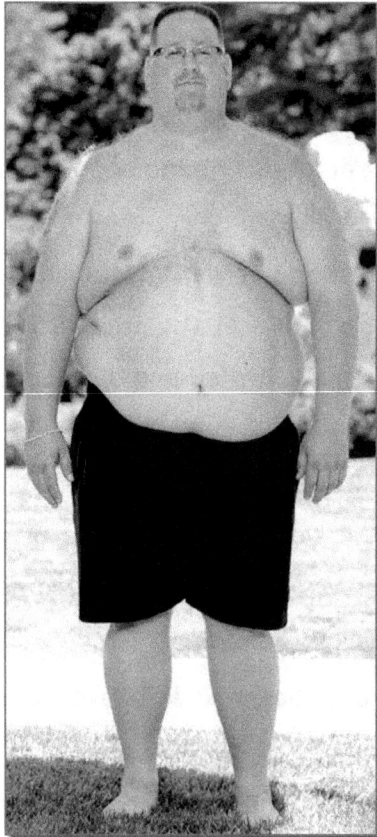

Bob Brenner at his biggest before becoming a cast member of ABC's **Extreme Weight Loss**.

While there are some important things about my weight loss journey that took me from that picture to 195 pounds in a single year, there was something even bigger that happened when I started to get my life in order. I realized how incredible my life really was!

Everybody has things that happen in their lives and, for some, those things are terrible and capable of sending a person straight to rock bottom. There are deaths of loved ones, frightening events, illnesses, and doubts of faith that occur every day in humanity. Other times, there may be a series of very little things that affect a person. These are the things that mess with our expected plans. Our tendency is to let them pile up and drag us down: a move, an unexpected newborn, a career change, and letting go of our "glory days."

With these little things in a person's day-to-day, he or she can begin to feel at the mercy of life's circumstances when really he or she is just a member of life, itself. We will all have messy experiences, but it's up to those living life to decide how to handle the mess.

I met so many people in my time on *Extreme Weight Loss* and in the years since the show, when working with fitness camps and in motivational speaking, who had triumphed over trials. I met men and women who had real problems and, again and again, I was discovering people who were succeeding *despite* circumstances and meeting goals *regardless* of obstacles. Illness, depression, addiction, abuse, and pain can all be overcome with the right attitude, the right first steps, and the right decisions when life calls an audible.

Much like weight is put on one pound at a time, so is the weight of the world. Both can come off with the right plan . . . a plan for living big, but not ugly.

By the time that the Raiders head coach, John Madden, retired from coaching, he had coached in the league for ten years, won a Super Bowl ring, would eventually be voted into the Pro Football Hall of Fame, and was the youngest coach ever to reach 100 victories. Amazingly, he was also just 42-years old.

We define ourselves far more than society ever will. Do not allow arbitrary assumptions of how you should handle struggles determine your path for you. If you have it in you to win, then, in Madden's words, *"Be a winner!"*

Live Big - Not Ugly!

Bruce Pitcher Ignites The Day!

When football went away, everything else did, too.

> "You can recognize survivors of abuse by their courage. When silence is so very inviting, they step forward and share their truth so others know they aren't alone."
>
> ~Jeanne McElvaney

Bruce Pitcher is about as unassuming as they come. When people meet this guy who always smiles and has an infectious life energy that seems to burst out of him against his will, they would never imagine the kind of hell he has had to overcome.

The first time Bob and Bruce met was at a casting call for **Extreme Weight Loss's** fourth season. Bob joined a group of potential cast members who had just seen his episode. He gave a motivational speech and shared that he had also been working as a football coach. While Bruce was a football coach, too, the two didn't initially click. Each thought the other didn't like him and shared the thought with show hosts, Chris and Heidi Powell.

At the three month mark for those who made the show, when all had their initial huge weight losses, Bob went out again to meet with the season four cast and encourage them toward their next goals. While the rest of the cast was excited, Bruce kept *"doing his own thing."*

Bruce ended up with a concussion and couldn't work out during that visit. Bob still didn't know him very well. He wanted to figure out if Bruce was being weak-minded about exercise. People want to find ways out of working out. Even when the weight loss is coming, it's hard to get motivated to coat hundreds of pounds of fat and skin in a blanket of salty sweat. As Bruce's year went along, Bob continued to check in with and motivate the people that were going through their weight transformations.

Neither knows what ultimately clicked, but when Bob and Bruce saw one another at the finale, they hit it off right away, as though they'd been friends during the whole year-long process.

"That Bob guy's awesome!" Bruce recounts, today.

From Left to Right: Bruce's (now) Fiancée, Alexa, Bruce Pitcher, Bob's wife, Kelly Brenner, and Bob Brenner. Slow, then fast friends!

When the two men were apart from the stress of the show and the pressure of meeting goals in front of an audience of millions, they realized they had a great deal in common and they maintained a friendship which has, since their *Extreme Weight Loss* experiences, only grown.

Then, came Destination Boot Camp. Bob and Bruce don't take for granted the great opportunity they received in being a part of *Extreme Weight Loss.* Before they had the kick start to their lifestyle changes through the reality show experiences, though, they had each been turned down multiple times for programs aimed at helping the morbidly obese handle real, tangible transformation.

Morbid obesity has to do with more than weight. It is effected by:

- Addiction
- Lifestyle
- Community
- Education
- Nutrition
- Motivation

This is where *Extreme Weight Loss's* Destination Boot Camp, sponsored by the Anschutz Health and Wellness Center, came in. People need more than just a diet. Transformation requires more than a workout plan, too! With Destination Boot Camp, people working toward large weight loss goals are motivated by people, like Bob and Bruce, who have been there and are still there, too, keeping the weight off in the real world.

Boot Campers are given an accountability community. They receive education in lifestyle and nutrition. They even have professionals on-hand to address the very real changes, not just physically and medically, but also emotionally and spiritually, that people face when going through a transformation. Transformation changes a person.

Essentially, Destination Boot Camp created the toolkit needed to make weight loss more than the latest flick of a yo-yo. Boot Campers gain a transformed lifestyle wherein healthy living has become the default choice.

Scan here to learn more about "Destination Boot Camp"
http://anschutzwellness.com/weight-loss/extreme-weight-loss-destination-boot-camp/

During Destination Boot Camp, Bruce and Bob, who were each invited to motivate others, talked a lot on the phone. They visited with cast members of **Extreme Weight Loss's** fifth season and they were able to bond and relate. Bruce began to see Bob as a mentor.

Bob Brenner and Bruce Pitcher at Destination Boot Camp in 2015.

Through Bruce's **Extreme Weight Loss** episode, as well as when the two men became friends following their reality television experiences, Bob discovered a great deal about Bruce's history as a football player.

If you ask Bruce how long he's played football, he answers, *'forever.'* He began in tackle football in the sixth grade, but—before then—it was flag football. In his hometown in Utah, there was no shortage of large, muscular, and tall players. A large Polynesian presence settled in the area meant that Bruce wasn't as big as some of the others, but he won the "Black Cat Award" for being the hardest worker on the team. He would play the scout team, go against varsity, and practice like crazy so that he could improve. By his senior year, on a line that averaged 285 pounds a guy, Pitcher earned his start. He could play any position he wanted, but fought for center.

The man who brought Bruce up through the ranks, taught him the game, coached him and his friends, and fostered a passionate love for the sport was his dad, Danny Pitcher. Danny Pitcher was everybody's favorite, loveable coach, but something else was going on behind the scenes and Bruce's entire future was going to be shaped by what happened, how he handled it, and the lessons he derived from the traumatic experience.

In 1999, Danny L. Pitcher was found guilty of a long list of charges related to his repeated sexual abuse of the young boys who were members of his teams. When the charges came, Bruce had been asked if he'd ever been hurt and, out of shame, embarrassment, pain, and even an undeserved obligation to protect his dad, he said, "No." Of all of the charges for which Danny Pitcher was convicted, the pedophilic acts against his own son were not among them. It would be years before Bruce said anything about being one of his father's victims.

It wasn't Bruce's past that defined him, though. It was how he *got* past – past all of it.

On a personal level, football saved Bruce's life. He had the camaraderie of team. The coaches took him under their wings. Despite his father, football stood for safety and acceptance. Ultimately, football *was* family for Bruce. He called his teammates brothers because that's who they were and that's what football stood for.

Football is the ultimate team game. Everybody has to rely on every single other person; it's a team effort. On a team, players are only as good as the last place guy. Football teaches its players to value everyone equally.

The other thing that football taught Bruce was that, even when the team didn't need him, he needed it.

Danny Pitcher coached a lot of Bruce's friends. He knew them all. They knew him. It was a huge ordeal, of course, as it should have been. The town had thought the world of the coach. When his dad was finally convicted, the newspaper article about his acts was brought to school. Bruce was a sophomore. Another student took a dump in his backpack. One kid transferred schools. Another quit football. Everybody knew who everyone else was . . . except for Bruce who didn't build up the courage to be honest about his abuse.

Bruce's team brothers stepped in and had the backs of *all* of the victims, including Bruce's. Things began to go smoother for him and he felt loved. It was that love that got him through. Love to Bruce was football that included community, hard work, and an openness to accept somebody who felt unacceptable.

Eventually, Bruce even opted to go into coaching, himself. He didn't coach to be like his dad, but like the coaches who had become father figures to him.

For Bruce, the lessons of football were the lessons that others gain from family.

> *"There's really no difference between team and family. In order for a family to function well, it needs to operate like a team. In order for a team to function well, it needs to operate like a family."*
> ~**Dave Strand** (*"Building A Championship Culture"*)

Today, Bruce Pitcher revels in his role as a youth football coach.

When football went away, everything else did, too. Bruce's friends went away on missions or school. He was trying to battle through his struggles when he had community and now that community was gone for Bruce.

Bruce had initially denied abuse to protect his father and, later, out of shame, but he realized how many more victims there were. He felt as though, if he had said something, they may have not been victims. Maybe it would have stopped with him. He had great friends who were great athletes and their lives were hard, at best, after what Danny Pitcher had done.

Bruce went on to graduate at 17-years old and head, as many from his hometown did, into mission work. He was one of the last to leave.

Looking back, he had merely been surviving. Between his mom, him, and his brothers, they just drifted day-by-day. Everything had been ripped from them in a whirlwind. He began to eat away his days and never thought about the weight. Those lessons of athleticism: the community, the hard work, the openness – he left those lessons behind when he went to the Mission Training Center.

"If I hear one more thing about this gospel, I'm going to throw this chair through the window," Bruce remembers saying during his training.

He was supposed to completely shut off the outside world and devote all of his time to the Lord. He couldn't do that; he needed community; Bruce came home early.

"What are you doing?" his mother asked. "You can't give God two years?" Bruce was told he should come home in a body bag, because he was going to end up like his father. Meanwhile, his father actually told him, from jail, that that the family would not be blessed because Bruce didn't go on the mission.

Bruce had nothing left. No football. No community. No mission. No family. No hope. He drank a big bottle of booze, and tried to kill himself by hanging, except – after years of food-addicted depression created a morbidly obese body, the belt broke.

Life post-athleticism for Bruce was about more than adjusting to life *off* the football field, it was about adjusting to life *on* a battlefield. He had been wounded. His brothers in arms had moved on. The man who *should* have been his commander in chief was actually his torturer. How could he take the crappy season that had been put before him and use the lessons of his athletic youth to get through and get better?

After the suicide attempt, a great therapist taught Bruce that he could live to the "poor me" life or go out and get the "for me" life. He just didn't know, yet, how to define "for me."

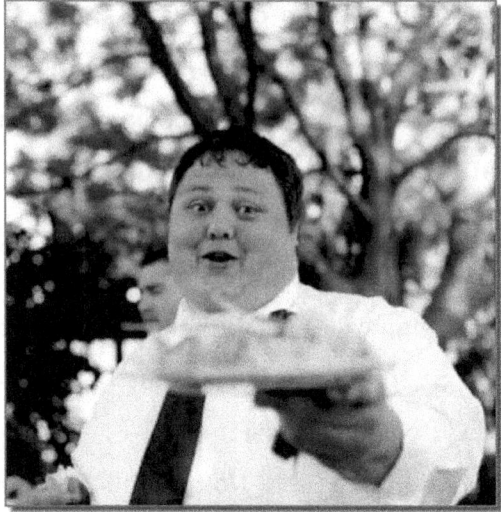

Food used to represent solace for Bruce.

While on his way to an all-you-can-eat buffet in Nevada, Bruce found out about an open-casting call for *Extreme Weight Loss*. Bruce had already unsuccessfully tried out for reality weight loss shows seven times. Because Bruce was ready to understand "for me," he didn't have anything to hold back.

Bruce remembers being asked, "Why should I pick you?"

"Me, my mom, and my brother deserve a break in life," he said.

His on-screen interview wasn't about weight; it was about getting off the battlefield. After the interview, Bruce waited.

At a local gas station, picking up foods he probably shouldn't eat, Bruce opened up an email on his phone from the show and, without finishing it, he saw the words, "Congratulations!" at the top.

He was so excited, he threw up.

The show was nervous to select Bruce because of his past. He was still broken. He needed therapy. In this new community, though, Bruce was accepted, again. It was a feeling he'd lacked since the end of his football playing days. The weight he'd gained had only been a side effect.

Once again, Bruce had community.

Once again, he was embroiled in the hard work required for success.

Bruce puts in the hard work with a fellow Camper at Destination Boot Camp

As for openness; here was an opportunity to finally change his life. This was what it was going to take to be happy. Bruce's inner athlete woke up with an appetite bigger than food could feed; it was an appetite for transformation.

Bruce's journey went beyond weight loss. As a victor over abuse, rather than a victim of it, he had somebody to face. With openness for the challenge, and a community to support him, Bruce was willing to put in the hard emotional work needed to confront Danny L. Pitcher, the father and coach who, in reality, did neither of those things for Bruce. In the midst of his weight transformation, he got that very opportunity when his father's parole hearing arose.

The night before his visit, Bruce was doing alright.
When he got to his house, the reality of the upcoming confrontation began to set in his mind.

When he actually drove to the prison, he realized emotionally what was really going down.

Bruce was told that he wouldn't be able to talk to his father. Instead, he listened while, for an hour and a half, the parole board read to Danny all of the things that he had done, grooming and abusing young boys and young men from 1980 until his conviction almost twenty years later. Then, without his expecting it, the judge asked if Bruce wanted to say anything. He realized that this was his chance; he could finally stand up to his dad. He wanted to make a wrong right. He wanted to speak for all of the victims he couldn't speak up for years ago and others who, maybe like him for so long, still hadn't said anything.

Bruce says that God lifted him up and gave him the words he needed to say that day. It was what was needed and if he had known he'd be called on, or if he'd gone over the words ahead of time, it wouldn't have been the right words. Shaking, and barely understandable through his tears, he uttered,

> *"I just wanted to say that I did love my dad with all my heart . . . I wanted to be a great son. It kills me to say this and, I'm sorry Dad, but I don't think he should get out. I think for his safety and others,*

he shouldn't get out. I just want to make a stand for all of the other victims he victimized that he thinks are okay. That's what I want to say today. Thank you."

Bruce didn't have just the weight of his obesity on him, he had the weight of the world. With the power of the positives from his athletic life, a life reignited during his weight loss transformation, he was able to accomplish amazing things. No matter what his struggles were or what had happened to him, he now saw his past as a blessing because it made him who he became. He stopped playing the victim card. He kept fighting and became a success . . . losing more than 200 pounds in a single year!

Bruce Pitcher at 382 pounds and, at the

*end of his transformation, at 181 pounds.
He's sporting a Raiders jersey from his buddy, Bob Brenner.*

Bruce had no idea what his episode would do for so many people. Getting to know Bob through Destination Boot Camp, he now speaks with him about how to live a victor's life and he believes he was meant to share his message, coach others, and make a positive impact.

Bruce and Bob take charge at Destination Boot Camp!

"With the opportunity I've been given through my transformation," he says, "it would be a slap in the face not to share my message."

Bruce's new message goes beyond the regained community, hard work, and openness lessons of his athletic years. When speaking with Bob, he gives applicable life skills that everybody can take, regardless of their athletic or non-athletic past and regardless of the struggles over which they have triumphed or from which they still carry the weight.

1. CHOOSE YOUR ATTITUDE!

Each day, we can look at our lives and choose whether we will be **victims** living in "poor me" pasts or **victors** working toward "for me" futures.

When Bruce was able to take off the true weight that had been in his life, not just the pounds, but the pains, his vision for the future became clear.

"Alexa and I will be a great couple," Bruce says of his fiancée. "Not only do we know about 'what not to do,' but we understand how to get through tough times."

2. IGNITE THE DAY!

When our alarms go off, do we fire up out of bed? Dowe jump up and give ourselves a little motivational speech?

"Let's do this one different," we should say to ourselves. "Let's do today better," we should say and we should say it every day.

There is no snooze button in life.

GET UP!

GET READY!

GET GOING!

Then, while going through our days, let's work to ignite other people's days, too. Many coaching programs have people list three positives or three gratitudes at the end of each day. In an ignited life, we can become those positives for others. What if we *shared* three positives with three others throughout our day? Imagine a world where purposefully positive people became the positive reflections of one another. We could do more than ignite a spark; we could start a wildfire of passionate encouragement.

3. TOUGHNESS

We need to be competitors in LIFE. Adversity? Smile at it. **Life happens. What are you gonna do about it?**

The toughness we feel on the field, when it's fourth and short – that's the toughness we need in life because it's always fourth and short. We're always trying to get that next first down. We're always making our way to the end zone and we're not scoring, we're losing.

To win life, Bruce Pitcher overcame tragically tough times. Today, he chooses to be a victor. He ignites every day and, with the integrity he recaptured long after his playing days, he brings toughness to a new field—the field of life—where he's winning big, but not ugly.

University of California, Berkley's Cal Bears Football team is most famously known for a comeback so incredible, it's simply referred to as, "the play." Stanford was ahead and the final play on the field appeared to leave the runner down. The Stanford band actually flooded the field only to discover that the Cal Bear runner was not down and he was coming right for them! Through the brass section, the Cal Bears scored the winning touchdown with an unintentional tackle to a Stanford trombone player!

Sometimes, we think we're winning when we're actually just setting ourselves up for a fall.

3

My Big Uglies had me living a L.I.E.

"We cannot always control everything that happens to us in this life, but we can control how we respond. Many struggles come as problems and pressures that sometimes cause pain. Others come as temptations, trials, and tribulations.
~L. Lionel Kendrick

When I look at the trials that my friend, Bruce Pitcher, had to overcome, my own struggles seem small and selfish by comparison. I think this is how many of us feel when we're working through the day-by-day issues. Why should we worry about a single late bill when we know other people in debts up to their eyeballs? Why should we be concerned about an extra ten pounds when we know a guy who is really fat? Why should we bother our minds with skipping some random family time for solo time when some people choose not to go home to their families at all at night?

The problem with this way of thinking is that the scales of our lives don't tip all at once. They tip little by little. Those ten pounds become ten more, then more, and, ultimately, you are the guy who is really fat. That bill becomes two bills, then several, then you are in debt. That one missed date or event, becomes several over a season, over a year, and ultimately you have a family that you don't know.

The answer to the problem is to ask HOW. How do we move from big, ugly lives to people who are ready to choose a positive attitude, ignite their days, and be tough enough to face our struggles? First, though, we have to recognize that there is a problem. We have to stop living lies.

- A *"L.ive Large" Life of Gluttony*
- A *Lifestyle of I.mbalance*
- A *Sense of E.ntitlement*

The selfish struggles I was living were really about the **L.ive Large** attitude from football that I kept even when football wasn't what was keeping my life on track.

During my growing years, it was my lifestyle that was extreme. Drinking, long hours, strip clubs, and big drug busts categorized a majority of my time spent. In those times, I ate and ate and ate, making my weight and my hate the unstoppable factors in my life.

~From "Live An Extreme Life"

When my scale was out of balance, it was really my lifestyle that was out of balance. I didn't realize that things were out of whack. I thought I was living the normal routine for a "guy's guy." Play football. Coach football. It was my passion. I love my family and my kids, but my passion was football. I felt that football had taught me so much about life that it needed to be on a pedestal. It was up high and everything else was below it.

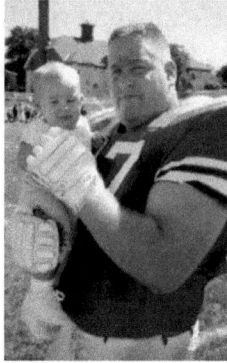

Not even fatherhood could steal Brenner's attention away from football. He's pictured here with his firstborn, Kayla.

I think that knowing your passion is important, but if you put one hundred percent of yourself into your passion, then *nothing* else in your life is being lived for. If you're not living for all parts of your life, then you're not bringing your whole, healthy self to that passion. Because you're not bringing a whole, healthy self to your passion, you don't do as well at it as you could. In turn, you think you need to give even more to what you love . . .

It's a vicious cycle and this was the second part of the L.I.E. I was living: a *Lifestyle of I.mbalance*.

What about doing something in your life with your relationships, faith, and friendships? If you're not making time for all of those other aspects in your life, you will end up tipping the scales toward living a lie.

For me, faith is a part of who I am when I'm winning in life. It's something bigger than I could ever be and never ugly. I start out my day reading my devotions. I get out of bed, grab my phone, and read my verse of the day. It sets my mind right for the plans in front of me. If I keep my life balanced on faith, all of the things that are difficult to face seem smaller and I'm able to always work toward better . . . even when I occasionally have to give up with feels "good."

> *Sacrifice is being willing to give up something good for something better.*
>
> *Life is full of boundless possibilities, but in order to transform a possibility into a reality we have to choose -- sacrificing the many in order to attain the one. Nothing is gained without something relinquished.*
>
> *Sacrifice has meaning only in the context of a goal, dream or mission. In pursuing these, we often face obstacles which require us to forfeit physical or emotional comfort in the service of something that matters more. Often, the greater the dream or vision, the greater the shared sacrifice required to attain it. Sacrifice is easier when we stay focused on what we are choosing rather than what we are giving up.*
>
> *~"Wisdom Commons"*

The Battle Against Imbalance

At the end of the day, faith is the most important thing in my life. I look to God and am thankful and appreciative. Whatever the words of my devotion say may just be a reminder of how to "set" my day.

I can be passionate about a lot of things, but I still have to make time to tell my wife every day that I love her, she's beautiful, and she's important.

If I don't address the other aspects in my life, I can't find balance in the rest of my life, nor can I find the energy and wholeness I need to *bring* passion to . . . to IGNITE on . . . those things that are important to me. The battle against imbalance begins by creating reminders and setting routines. You need to identify the three to five things that you are most passionate about and that are lacking your attention. Then, come up with a means of making the routines for those things into rituals that you crave.

*The **Battle to Defeat Imbalance**, therefore, is:*

*1 – **Identify** the important purpose in your life.*

*2 – Set a **Reminder** to be sure that important purpose is getting your attention.*

*3 – Create a **Routine** for serving the purpose on a regular basis.*

*4 – Develop a **Ritual** around the routine by tying it to an additional source of passion or purpose.*

For me, the things I identified as purposes included fitness, finances, faith, friends, and family. Take a look at my battle plan:

1 - FITNESS is an important, healthy thing for me to maintain in my life.

Reminder – Set out workout clothes the night before so that they look at me in the morning.

Routine – Put the workouts on the calendar on a regularly maintained schedule.

Ritual – Share in the exercise with my wife so that it is not just a workout, but a bonding time that we each look forward to having.

2 - FINANCES are necessary to future planning and present security.

Reminder – Set up accounts to receive income.

Routine – Have the money direct deposited into the various accounts and account types at each pay period.

Ritual – Tie some of the accounts to education, vacation, and special services. When the money is for a long-term goal, like college for yourself or a child, you feel a sense of investing rather than just saving. Saving for retirement can feel the same way, especially if you add a layer of vision planning with your family. If you pour money into saving for a mission trip or to support a cause you believe in, you have moved from the routine of setting aside money to the ritualistic service of others.

3 - FAITH is the foundation for my own life and the purposes I try to achieve within it.

<u>Reminder</u> – Make church a calendar appointment.

<u>Routine</u>– Go to church each week.

<u>Ritual</u> – Share the church experience with your family and follow up the teachings with a study in a small group, on a mission trip or service project, or even in discussions with family and friends.

4 - FRIENDS were always a part of my life when I was living big, but I needed to find a way to keep those connections without also being ugly.

<u>Reminder</u> – Catch up with friends over coffee.

<u>Routine</u> – Choose to schedule something purposeful on get-togethers such as a bike ride or workout.

<u>Ritual</u> – Use the time together to be accountable in one another's lives. Promote the time to quality time, discussing one another's lives and talking about the difficult things that maybe are difficult to share. Give your time together deeper meaning by talking with one another about the good, the bad . . . and the ugly.

5 – FAMILY. It's at the heart of who I am, now. I made family a <u>reminder</u>, a <u>routine</u>, and a <u>ritual</u> across every other thing I did. They became a part of my fitness, a part

of my finances, a part of my faith, and the ones I talk about with my closes friends.

Your own top three or five areas of passion may be different than mine, but you still need to align them with a reminder, a routine, and a ritual if you are seeking to maintain that passion and ignite on it!

You also have to be willing to admit that the change is needed.

We don't talk about pride and how negative it is in our lives. I was finally over my pride. Finally, I was smart enough to see my addictions to food and alcohol and how these things were ruining every aspect of my life. I needed help with food and nutrition. That's what everybody could see, but those were just the weaknesses that were on display. Those were the fails that everybody noticed. I hid all of the other things. The weight was really an addiction to food. I was an alcoholic. My relationships were hanging on by a string . . . and my pride was holding a pair of scissors to that string.

My selfishness was unstoppable. I was keeping up appearances instead of keeping up on budgets, being the fun guy instead of the reliable husband, and laughing off the weight that could kill me.

I was extreme; I was unstoppable; and I was on the path to a soul that would break at an early age if I didn't find better areas in my life to apply those words, to gain something besides failures, and to lose something besides myself.

In order to Ignite in your life, you need to put to bed the *Sense of **E.ntitlement*** – the "E" of the L.I.E. that is so easy to miss when it shows up little by little. There is no given in life. Sometimes you have to work harder than other people. I ended up here; having to work harder because I hadn't for so long.

Until you get rid of life's little by little lies, you'll never truly get to live big.

In each of his stints as a head coach in the NFL, with the Eagles, Rams, and Chiefs, Dick Vermeil took over teams with losing records and eventually led them to double digit win seasons and appearances in the playoffs.

Every morning, we can redefine our big futures. We alone are in charge of choosing our turnaround moments and executing them.

Live Big - Not Ugly!

Vince Papale's Invincible Moments!

*E*very year, a few more branches.

Winners embrace hard work. They love the discipline of it, the trade-off they're making to win. Losers, on the other hand, see it as punishment. And that's the difference.
~Lou Holtz

Vince and Bob met three years after Bob's weight loss transformation. The two bonded over the lives of football, hard work, and sharing positive messages in their post-athletic lives. When it came to talking about Bob's decision to lose the weight and gain his purpose in life, Vince said to Bob, "That was your Invincible Moment."

Invincible; *incapable of being conquered*

Moment: *a definite period or stage*

Vince knew something about definite stages in which a person couldn't be conquered. He lived a few of them!

Vince Papale's first football team was the Glendale Heights Ownership Association as a Glendale Indian. It was a neighborhood team started by his dad, a first generation immigrant to the World War II neighborhood where Papale grew up. Vince wasn't a particularly big guy, so he was nearly conquered many times. In junior high school, he was told he was too light to play. By the ninth grade, Vince was still less than five feet tall and didn't even weigh 100 lbs. He played junior high school football, nonetheless, under George Corner who became a mentor for life.

INVINCIBLE MOMENT:

When dealing with mental illness of his mother, Corner enabled Vince to find strength. He visited her when she was not well and offered the emotional support that was lacking when his mother was gone. Vince's Dad became his best friend, but the emoting came from George Corner.

Once in high school, size mattered to the former Marine Drill Sergeant Cunningham who coached at that level with a frightening demeanor. It appeared (for the first time) that his playing days for football could be done. Papale moved to soccer, track, and baseball, where he excelled due to his speed.

INVINCIBLE MOMENT:

Lucky for Vince, Corner came up to the high school level before he graduated and he allowed him to go out for the team. He was still small, but he'd grown enough to not get crushed on the field . . . and he could run, so they couldn't catch him to do the crushing.

At five foot seven and 145 pounds, he became the primary receiver to a leading quarterback. The two killed it on the field.

Vince got the flavor.

He wanted more football.

It would be awhile before that taste would be satisfied. College wouldn't come calling for him as a football player, so Vince faced the second time his playing days might be done. Having proven himself on the pole vault to the tune of records and championships, Vince was given a track scholarship to St. Joe's, a college that didn't even have a football team.

"Happy Father's Day, Dad," he'd told his father. "We're going to St. Joe's."

INVINCIBLE MOMENT:

Vince became a five-event man on St. Joe's Track team. He was a natural-born, gifted athlete who'd had great coaches and mentors to help get him to the moments in which he could excel and ignite!

George Corner shared with Vince a quote from Cardinal Leon J. Suenes *"Happy are those who dream dreams and are willing to pay the price to make them come true."* Hard work remained part of Vince's battle plan for everything that came his way.

Life came calling, as it does for most people, after college finished for Vince. He dabbled in semi-professional football in the Seaboard, and later World Football Leagues, but mostly he spent his time teaching and coaching at the same school that had given him his glory days of football.

Vince still today tells young groups to give thanks to their coaches and teachers. They are the first responders. That is essentially the reason he graduated and ended up teaching back at his Alma Mater, teaming up with Coach Corner and becoming the best and closest of friends with the man who was once his mentor.

Vince got married, went to work, and was satisfied with life. The idea of ever really making it in the world of football was a far-fetched reality for Vince as age thirty snuck up on him. For the third time, that life seemed to be in the past.

INVINCIBLE MOMENT:

That's when the surreal life came calling in the form of not-yet-at-that-time legendary coach Dick Vermeil. Vince's short stint with the World Football League captured Vermeil's attention and Vince Papale, who was eight to twelve years older than the average rookie, was given a chance to become a Philadelphia Eagle.

Training camp was sadistic.

There were no shortcuts.

There was no substitute for hard work

Hard work had to be quality.

It was hard work with a purpose.

A miracle happened for Vince. He became America's Cinderella story . . . a local teacher getting to play for the team he'd cheered on all his life.

Philadelphia Eagle #83, Vince Papale (1976-1978)

As grateful as Vince was and still is to this day for the opportunity to be an Eagle, it didn't come easily. Vermeil was famous among his players for saying, "You don't ever drown in sweat," an old line from coaching great, Lou Holtz.

Vince had surgery on his separated right shoulder at the end of his third year as an Eagle. When he returned for the following year's pre-season, he re-separated his right shoulder and dislocated his left in the same day. He moved to the Eagles' injured reserve.

That's when Vince tried to take advantage of his next invincible opportunity. He had a career with CBS lined up, and he started training in network broadcasting in New York. Because of contract issues, the entire television move ended up falling through. He had the perfect transition going, but it didn't take off and it was gone at the same time that injury took him out of the game he loved . . . and this time it wouldn't come calling, again.

It was a new kind of hard for Vince.

He ended up divorced.

He had a good job, but it was one that he hated.

In an attempt to regain passion, he took a seventy percent cut in pay and got back in radio to try to work his way back into television. It didn't happen.

He managed to get back on his feet, though struggling financially, but the divorce killed him emotionally and Vince moved into a self-destructive mode. He became a man who felt purposeless and hopeless.

He didn't feel invincible.

He didn't have anything to ignite on.

He didn't have a battle plan.

INVINCIBLE MOMENT:

Then, he met Janet Cantwell at a charity event and Vince decided to plug back into the world. Janet, the oldest of nine, lived by the mantra "just one more," a hard work lesson that carried her all the way to the U.S. National Gymnastics Team and an Olympic alternate. Janet was the little engine that could. She was Vince's "just one more," and she would be the last one more he would ever need.

"I wouldn't be alive right now if it weren't for Janet," Vince insists.

When Vince's daughter, Gabriella was born, Vince felt grounded . . . calm . . . for the first time since his world came tumbling down. Her heartbeat on her first sonogram was like a northern star to Papale and he immediately wanted another. Three years later, Vince and Janet welcomed Vinnie.

"My kids will never be told they're not good enough," he insists.

Vince planted a holly tree outside a beautiful window in their home for their Gabriella. It was a gift to her and it's grown, just like her. It used to be just two-feet tall and now it fills his view, as his children fill his heart. Every year, he spots a few more branches. It's like life that way. The branches are forever even when leaves fall off and new ones come.

Football was a leaf that fell.

His first marriage was a leaf that fell.

Vince is still growing, though.

Today, Papale coaches his son, Vinnie, who he coached throughout his life. He tries not to wear the coach hat in the house or the dad hat on the field. He doesn't get paid, but when a parent or kid gives him a hug and says they love him, it keeps him going. It keeps him igniting, battling on, and seeking Invincible Moments.

Coaching, for Vince, is bonding and it's connecting. It's teaching those young players the same lessons Vince had to learn later through "Just One More" Janet: There is no shame in failure. We're in an instant coffee world with a lack of patience and discipline, but—as Dick Vermeil would agree—there are no shortcuts for hard work.

In everything Vince accomplished in life, he recognizes a feeling of strength from his athletic experience and that strength was given by his parents and the community around him. It's an attitude that prevails – an attitude that says, "You can be down, but you can never be out."

- In 1976, Papale was nicknamed "Rocky" by his teammates.
- In 1998, the made for television movie, *"The Garbage Picking Field Goal Kicking Philadelphia Phenomenon"* was inspired by Papale.
- Disney™, in 2006, just dubbed him *"Invincible"* in a major motion picture of the same title (and inspired by the book telling his story).

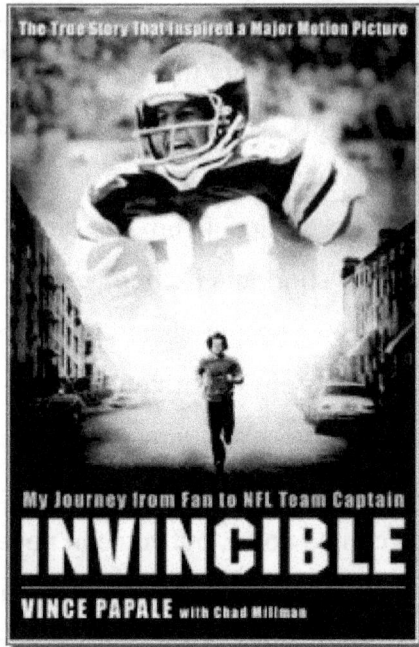

The True Story That Inspired a Major Motion Picture

My Journey from Fan to NFL Team Captain

INVINCIBLE

VINCE PAPALE with Chad Millman

Vince Papale's book that inspired the movie starring Mark Wahlberg.

This last title seems the most fitting. Again and again in Vince's life, he has used the lessons of athleticism to become unconquerable in life's defining stages. He has created and *lived* Invincible Moments.

"It's about what you need to do. Understand and know the challenge. Know who you are. Make sure you have your game plan to go, not from A to B, but from A to Z. Know your dream and finish it."

At the end of the Disney movie portraying a chapter from Vince Papale's life, Papale looks at the man lined up in front of him and realizes that, while he pretends to be charging, he had no weight on his fingers. He read the knuckles of the man in front of him and knew they had to move quickly to change their approach.

"Check Zoro! Check Zoro!" he called to his teammates. They needed to change their plan.

The bodies shifted, the ball was off and, in mere *Invincible Moments*, the Eagles were scoring a winning touchdown.

Vince has since moved from glory days to a life of glory based on his "Three A Lessons" from those days:

1. **Analyze** – Read life's play in front of you.
2. **Adapt** – Make the changes you need to win.
3. **Achieve** – Do what you have to do to get it done.

Vince shares his three A's with audiences around the country using the messages from "*Invincible*," and a follow-up book, *"Be Invincible: A Playbook for Reaching Your Full Potential"* written with Janet and their co-author Tim Vandehey.

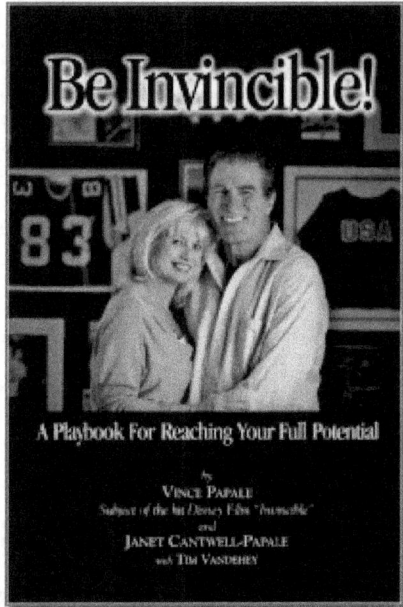

Be Invincible!

A Playbook For Reaching Your Full Potential

by
VINCE PAPALE
Subject of the hit Disney Film "Invincible"
and
JANET CANTWELL-PAPALE
with TIM VANDEHEY

Coach Dick Vermeil wrote the forward for
Papale's second book, "Be Invincible."

Scan here to purchase Invincible Books
http://www.vincepapale.com/invinciblebooks.html

-

In life, Vince has been down, but he uses football's big lessons to make sure he's never out and never ugly.

Down 15 - 16 to the Buffalo Bills in the 1999 AFC Wildcard game, the Titans were receiving the ball with just sixteen seconds to go in the game. Neal received, but immediately handed off to Wycheck, who the defense was on right away. Before they arrived, though, Wycheck got off a lateral to Dyson. It was Dyson who ran in the winning touchdown! The trick play has become known as "The Music City Miracle."

Transitions aren't always clean or predictable, but—if played right— they can carry you to victory. What miracles are waiting on the other sides of your transitions?

4

*T*he field changes.

"Life is one big transition"

~Willie Stargell

I chose a new attitude.

I recognized the lie.

I had my Invincible Moment . . . the moment that told me it was time for change.

Change alone isn't enough to earn success, though. What's important is not just changing what isn't working, but transitioning to what will work and we will each need to identify, for ourselves, what will get us through that transition between our comfortable selves, and the selves we were meant to be.

The field changes.

Constantly.

We need a strong enough "why" in our lives to carry us to the next plays in front of us.

At the start of my weight transformation, I wanted to get healthy. It was a simple *external why.* An external why is a person's public why.

"Bob, why did you decide to lose the weight?" people would ask and it's something I felt comfortable speaking about in front of anybody.

Scan here to get a glimpse into Bob's speaking career.
https://youtu.be/dzFJLrQ_yYU

"I want to be healthier for my family. I want to be healthier for my wife, for my kids, for coaching, and for my job as a cop."

Maybe an external why even starts to brush on some of the emotional connections we make to our choices.

"I want to fit into a seat in the theater. I want be able to ride in an airplane. I want to be comfortable in my car."

These kinds of statements may be true, but it doesn't mean that they tell the whole story. These were my socially acceptable whys. An external why, or many of them, don't take much work to come up with. You could sit down and, as easily as a pro and con list, come up with very true, yet very incomplete, reasons for making a positive transition.

External whys can light a spark, but without an internal why, it could fizzle out. Internal whys go beyond those thoughts and feelings we could flippantly offer to questions about our transformations and transitions. Internal whys are those sorts of things that, if shared at all, are only shared with the non-judging "superfriends."

The external whys of purpose are the outer layers. It's necessary to peel back that onion to understand the deeper reason behind your purpose. That internal why is what really drives change. It gets to your core. It's the heart of what would keep you motivated to make changes long term.

"I want to stop being tempted."

"I'm tired of being tired."

"I'm embarrassed."

"I'm ashamed."

An external why is easy. An internal why requires sitting down and doing some soul searching. Knowing your whys is how to manage the journey through transitions.

The first transition that really stands out for me was going to college at age 17. I was leaving home and, though I didn't know it then, I'd never live there again. I felt directionless. I had no financial foundation. I went from dependent to independence.

TRANSITION: FROM HOME TO COLLEGE

TIMING:

- I was young, unconfident, and unprepared.
- It wasn't my own timing.
- The daily time I had was preordained by seasons and classes.

INTELLECT:

- Minimal intellect was forced.
- My main goal was athleticism.
- I had to maintain a 2.0 in order to be eligible to play football.

UNITY:

- My unity moved from my home to my team.
- Unity revolved around a support group made up of football and fraternity brothers.

During this transition, I had a book of *external whys*: I wanted the college experience; I wanted the competitive level of football; I wanted to create those glory days.

Without an *internal why* driving my college life, though, this transition was burdened with the *Big Uglies* of: heavy drinking, commitment issues, and a lack of integrity.

TRANSITION: FROM SINGLE LIFE TO MARRIED PARENTHOOD

TIMING:

- I didn't get to adjust to marriage before I was thrust into parenthood.
- I had only six months from married to married with children.
- Kelly and I went just three years from our first date to our first child.

INTELLECT:

- I quit college after earning 100 college credits
- I was only one year from my Bachelor's Degree, but I had to give up school because I needed to provide for my family.

UNITY:

- I didn't know that my unity had to change.
- I went from playing football to coaching football.

- My team was still my primary family.

My *external whys* were all related to image. I wanted to look the part of the grown up who had gotten down the routine of this adulthood thing, and succeeded at it. I had attained a beautiful wife, and our first child, while keeping my "fun" life intact. Without an *internal why* driving me to be the best husband and father I could be, my single to married parenthood transition was burdened with the *Big Ugly* of broken priorities.

TRANSITION: FROM COLLEGE LIFE TO WORKING LIFE
TIMING:

- Fresh on the heels of youth, I had the drive and determination to work my way up through the department, from Jailer, to Deputy Sheriff, to Detective, to a specialized Narcotics Force.
- I was newly married and presumed my role was only about being a financial provider
- My daily time was full of long, hard hours that I didn't run past my wife, Kelly and any minutes left over were dedicated to, what else? Coaching football.

INTELLECT:

- At each career level I went through, I became proficient and really learned the trade.

- I passionately studied for each next step through interviews, mentoring, asking others about their experiences, and preparing for the job duties of the next level.
- I ended every interview by saying, "Thank you. I'm the best candidate for this.

UNITY:

- I was forever going to be a part of the brotherhood of the police force.

My *external whys* seemed innocuous on the surface. I wanted to do well in my career and provide well for my family. I was single-minded, though, just as I had been with football. I didn't have *internal why* for the purposes behind advancing or caring for my loved ones. My transition to work was burdened with the *Big Ugly* of the consuming manner in which it took over my entire life.

TRANSITION: FROM A SELFISH LIFE TO A FAITH-GUIDED ONE

TIMING:

- Timing was perfect, of course. It wasn't my own timing. It was God's timing.
- I was ready to hear a new message and discover my internal whys.

INTELLECT:

- I needed to be open to learning and exploring what faith would really mean to me.
- I needed to be willing to learn about personal relationship.
- I needed to immerse myself in a new way of doing everything I'd ever done.

UNITY:

- I had unity with a God I came to know.
- Unity with God enabled me to improve on and have unity in all of my other relationships, rather than just the select brotherhoods I had prioritized over loved ones all my life.

My *external whys* of the past transitions seemed small. Everything I had been striving toward in my life was external. How did I look to the outside world? I had been in charge of my own life and that prideful ego was what drove everything, from how I treated my family, to where I placed my priorities. For the first time in my life, I recognized the truth of these external whys and was ready to invest in an *internal why*. I had been shown great grace, somehow maintaining (although, poorly) the roles and relationships in my life. I owed something back and the only *Big Ugly* left burdening my life was me . . . 448 lb., alcoholic, food-addicted, bankrupt, admittedly broken me.

I was ready for the transition to a weight loss transformation that was as big as my mindset transformation and that left behind the uglies of my past.

Life's field always is changing – always transitioning. We move from the playful fields of our youth, to school fields, and work fields, and fields on which we have to do battle against the forces, both external and internal, that are holding us back from our greater purposes. If we're lucky, one of those transitions are Invincible Moments for us.

We need transition plans, laden—not just with the external whys that the world approves; not just with timing, intellect, and unity—but the internal whys, the engines that ignite us toward victory on life's battlefields.

The Seattle Seahawks, under Coach Pete Carroll, were Super Bowl contenders two years in-a-row, taking the title for Super Bowl XLVIII. Winning with a smile, Carroll follows the advice of his mother, treating every day as if something positive were about to happen.

It's as important to keep your mind motivated in a transformation as it is to keep your body motivated.

Live Big - Not Ugly!

Dr. Holly's Mental Mindset!

The body follows the mind.

I wanted to run out of that tunnel to prove to everybody that I worked . . . that I was somebody.
~Daniel "Rudy" Ruettiger

Dr. Holly Wyatt, affectionately donned, simply, "Dr. Holly" and Brenner met during the fourth season of **Extreme Weight Loss**. While Bob was on-hand as a motivator, with Dr. Holly as the medical expert for show, it was the latter who continued work in Bob's transformed life to discover the secrets of a positive mental mindset.

Trained as an endocrinologist and having worked at the University of Colorado for twenty-three years, Dr. Holly specializes in bodyweight regulation and obesity intervention. Early in her life, Holly realized that she had to work a lot harder than her friends to stay healthy. In college, and later in medical school, she gained a lot of weight. She realized, in the midst of her studies, that she was interested in the specialty. She had some insights and knew that she wanted to bring a new voice to the growing field.

There are a lot of reasons that one person might gain weight more easily than another:

1. GENETICS – Some people do have a natural predisposition toward higher weight or higher fat to lean muscle ratios. It means they *will* have to work harder. It doesn't mean they can't achieve their weight loss goals; they just have to do more.

When Holly was on a dance squad in Texas, she had to weigh in every week and, if the dancers weighed more than 135lbs, they were out. She saw other dancers able to eat cookies and pizza, but she had to be perfect in her diet, in order to maintain that "ideal" dancer weight. She had a genetic predisposition to a less lean body.

Some people are dealt cancer cards; she had weight cards. She had to work to be the best she could be.

2. ENVIRONMENT – Maybe it's the home you grew up in, the rituals you keep with friends, or the workplace you go to every day that has an office stocked with doughnuts and birthday cakes. If you are in an environment in which healthy choices are limited, nutritious ones are vacant, and model health behaviors are not modeled, you are automatically in a handicapped position for overcoming a weight loss challenge.

3. BEHAVIORS – Making choices to be sedentary, while maintaining high-calorie diets will eventually lead to unhealthy weight gain, or—at a minimum—the cardiopulmonary and respiratory issues that result from inactive lifestyles. Regardless of your natural body type and even if you grow up in and then maintain an ideal nutrition and fitness environment, you have the power, through the behaviors you choose, to either ignite or stunt your own health transformation.

Genetics may load the gun on obesity, but it is environmental and behavioral factors that have the power to pull the trigger.

In her decades of experience dealing with extreme weight loss transformations, countless individuals have asked to know Wyatt's top three tips (or number one piece of advice, or the ten things that one needs to know, etc.) for nutrition and activity. While those things are, indeed, important to know, they're not the critical or missing pieces necessary to successful transformation.

Dr. Holly imparts wisdom on a group of Destination Boot Campers.

As Bob has successfully discovered in the years that have passed since his own 56% weight loss, losing weight is a far different animal than keeping it off. One reason why people fail, finding themselves in lose-regain-lose-regain-lose-regain cycles, is that they don't understand the difference. The skill set for maintenance is not the same as the skill set for losing. You need to understand the difference if you're going to succeed.

For initial loss, Nutrition is driving the car. It's hard to be successful without paying attention to diet. There are actually multiple diets to get a person to his or her goal. Use common sense in selection. It's not really a magic formula. More natural foods, more lean protein, and more vegetables with a decrease in processed foods, sugar, and unhealthy fats will get a person there. It's not about *what* diet is used,so much as that there is a diet; there is a structure. Especially if "your gun is loaded," you have to have a structured eating plan.

Once weight loss has been attained, the transformed person moves to maintenance mode; physical activity is in the front seat and nutrition is now in the back. Activity preserves muscle mass (which is better for metabolism), as well as heart health. In addition, physical activity will provide more than a healthy *appearance*, it will help to maintain healthy organs and body functionality – true health. Just as your motivation should be both external and internal, so should be what you are motivated toward!

When a person is on a journey working toward an extreme weight loss, both diet and fitness will be vital in the losing process. Both must be dialed in, but a person can't keep the exact nutrition (or fitness levels) of that initial loss maintained indefinitely. An achievable structure must be put in place, in order to maintain the goal once it has been attained.

Those tidbits of advice Dr. Holly shares about weight loss, weight maintenance, nutrition, and activity are not groundbreaking new evidence for successful transformation. Where she really sets herself apart, though, is on the science of positivity. It's a science that's hard to measure. Association studies, by Chapel Hill's Barbara Frederickson, to name one, provide some insight on the matter. Frederickson's studies don't prove cause (positivity) and effect (success), but they do show association between the two areas. These studies give the idea that, when there are higher levels of positivity, people live longer, don't feel as cold, and have lower blood pressure, to name a few associations.

Other studies show that there are additional effects, such as an increase of the broadening effect. An individual is able to see more possibilities and opportunities; he or she has better brainstorming. Performing a positive mindset exercise before going into a brainstorming session, versus going negatively into brainstorming, has shown the result of coming up with more ideas.

While it may seem tangential, Dr. Holly believes that a positive mental mindset is vitally important to weight management. If a person approaches transformation with a mental barrier to the gym because of embarrassment or to food because he or she is easily tempted, it is the mental battle, and not the physical battle, that wields the sword that could cut the transformation off at the knees. Creating a positive mindset will broaden the mind to creative solutions for achieving success. Instead of asking, *IF* he or she can succeed, the person is more likely to ask *'HOW can I make this work?'*

If you want to build a muscle in the gym, you do repetitive exercises. We don't do a single curl to build a bicep. It needs to be used in exponential repetitions and increasing weight. Only then will the muscle get bigger. Think of the mind as a muscle. The body follows the mind. It's important to work on the mindset. There is no cutting of corners. Her lessons have been widely implemented in Wyatt's book, "State of Slim," in which she teaches readers to:

- **Reignite your metabolism** by reigniting your fat burning engine, you will lose weight and have more energy.

- **Rebuild your metabolism** by training your metabolism to adjust to different fuel sources and lose 20 pounds in just 8 weeks.
- **Reinforce your metabolism** by continuing to lose weight and solidify a new lifestyle and mindset to support your success!

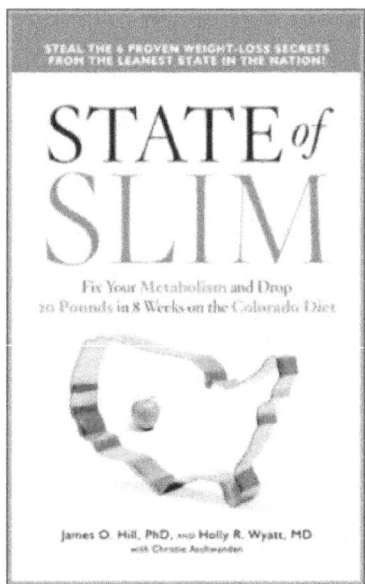

Dr. Holly R. Wyatt's book was written with
Dr. James O. Hill and Christie Aschwanden

It's no surprise that Wyatt has been successful in working with people such as Bob Brenner and Bruce Pitcher. She believes athletes have an advantage beyond their past physical experiences, even if it was from school days. While they may have fallen out of some of their habits, they have the mindset.

Wyattcan fix the diet and activity, but she also works to reawaken that mindset of positivity, visualization, expected success, a hard work attitude, and delayed gratification. These are the real skills that have to be pulled out and it's easier to get out a muscle that's been used before, as opposed to starting from scratch.

Scan here to purchase
"State of Slim"
http://www.stateofslim.com/

There are activities that strengthen a person's mental muscle and make it more emotionally resilient. The mind learns to bend without breaking, just as a muscle in the body. Dr. Holly Wyatt teaches the practice of:

MENTAL MINDSET EXERCISES
GRATITUDE:

- Practice every morning by saying those things for which you are grateful.

- Adjust your mindset for your entire day.
- Daily practice changes the wiring in your brain to recognize your gratitudes.

DEVELOP INTERNAL MOTIVATIONS:

- The best "what" blueprint is not helpful without a strong enough "why" to achieve it.
- Why is of equal importance to WHAT.
- Hook internal whys to the new behaviors required for your goal to gain a push.

Internal motivators are deeper, private whys and they are the most powerful driving forces to our goals. If you can figure out what the internal whys are to you, they will get you up at 4:00 in the morning with a wake-up call. They will drive your behavior.

External motivators are important and powerful too. Things such as money, clothing, and competitions provide quick, short term wins in life.

External motivators are the gasoline in our engines. They burn, but quickly. Internal motivators are the coals that, once heated, will keep the fire lit for those long-term successes. A strong transformation plan uses both. A little gasoline is okay, but you have to be developing coals.

IDENTIFY CORE VALUES:

- By tying to something that's really important to you, you will continue toward success

- Decide how you want to live, and be, and feel!
- Connect to something larger than yourself (maybe by doing a brainstorm to focus on that "broadening" effect).
- By believing in something bigger, a person becomes, not just more mentally resilient, but more emotionally resilient.

There are tools for laying out the mental plan of transformation. Everybody is different, just like physical plans and nutritional plans. The work for positivity is achieved through gratitude, internal motivators, and emotional resiliency achieved through core value identification. True success stories in transformation have done the work of tending the mental garden. They pull the weeds. They water the areas that are in need of sustenance. They do the planting of new ideas and exercises. They keep at it. They fertilize it with short term achievements as they work toward long-term goals.

Whether the Big Ugly in a person's life is related to weight, addiction, dependency, or grief, if he or she works to tend the field where the transformation takes place, the battle through it will stand a greater chance of being won. Through mental exercises, people undergoing transformations can live big and not ugly.

In 2002, motivated by the September 11th terrorist attacks on U.S. soil, brothers Pat and Kevin Tillman gave up prestigious, well-paying professional careers in the NFL and MLB, respectively, to join the enlisted ranks of the military and defend their country. The two literally gave up teammates on playing fields for an elite unit on battlefields because a bigger WHY was calling.

When you identify your bigger why, are you ready to make the changes necessary to go after it?

4

Read the play in front of you.

"We accept the verdict of the past until the need for change cries out loudly enough to force upon us a choice between the comforts of further inertia and the irksomeness of action."

~Louis L'amour

It was kind of special to transition from a local high school to the Carroll College football family. At our homecoming game in 1988, we were undefeated and playing the five-time national championship football team. The (also) undefeated Augustana was coming to us in little Waukesha, Wisconsin.

Years later, I was able to look back and realize how special and remarkable that game and that season were. Ten thousand people watched from the grass, along the hills around our field, and even in the road. Media coverage from all over the place was there. It was a big deal. I didn't really think much about it at the time, but it ultimately be the biggest game I'd ever be a part of.

On the second play of the game, one of our offensive linemen called an audible. Sometimes, players give a dummy call. They say a word, but it means nothing. I thought my teammate had made a dummy call. He wanted me to block down to the guy inside of me on a pass play. I didn't block and, because that player was unblocked, he sacked our quarterback. It was the only sack I ever gave up in my career and it was on the biggest game in my life. We won 24-21, but it's that play that I remember most of all..

Read the play in front of you. It's important to adjust to the opponent in front of you on a game-by-game basis and play-by-play basis. You "read the knuckles," as Papale would say, and—in milliseconds—decide if you need to make a change.

Two and a half decades after that Carroll-Augustana game, I was reading the play in front of me. It was change. I needed to eradicate the Big Ugly . . . the big *me* . . . from my life with the lessons of my Big Ugly days.

TIMING:

- Timing was ideal. I was open to change.
- My weight loss came as the second most perfect timing in my life; faith came first which set my heart right for the transformation timing.

INTELLECT:

- I had a new understanding of internal and external whys and was able to apply this new knowledge to drive me through the transition, focusing on the gasoline of short-term weight loss goals and the coal of long term lifestyle maintenance.

UNITY:

- I had unity with a family for whom I had changed.

I had unity with a new community unified by purpose including inspirational friends going through similar struggles. My weight change had to be about so much more than how it looked on me. Daily, I would spend time in study and found that Max Lucado often shared the wisdom I was seeking to live in this new life.

A woman battles with depression. What's the solution suggested by some well-meaning friend? Buy yourself a new outfit! A husband is in an affair that brings him as much guilt as it does adventure. The solution? Hang out with people who don't make you feel guilty. Change your style. Get a new haircut. Case after case of treating the outside while ignoring the inside.

And the result? The woman gets a new outfit, and the depression disappears...for a day, maybe. The husband finds a bunch of buddies who sanction his adultery. The result...peace, until the crowd's gone. Then the guilt is back. The exterior polished, the interior corroding. The outside altered, the inside faltering. One thing is clear. Cosmetic changes are only skin deep!

Jesus said, "Blessed are the pure in heart" (Matthew 5:8). And the message of the Beatitude is a clear one. You change your life by changing your heart!

~Max Lucado, "The Applause of Heaven"

In many ways, this time in my life was the end of the Big Uglies. I went beyond cosmetic changes to drop the crap that came along with me from the football field: heavy drinking, commitment issues, a lack of integrity, broken priorities, all-consuming neglect of my loved ones, alcoholism, food-addiction, bankruptcy, and brokenness.

In other ways, it was a reawakening to the Big Uglies . . . those lessons from my athletic days that I had distorted for so many years.

My *timing* had been poisoned with my *"L.ive Large"* *Life of Gluttony.*

"I've heard stories about you," some of the new detectives of the Metropolitan Drug Unit said to me when I returned to close out my career there after a stint on daytime detective work. "You're all parties and strip joints. It's legend."

I thought about all of the nights at home that I missed with my kids when they were growing up and all of the years of bonding I missed with my wife. My time had been dedicated to growing myself.

"Enjoy the rest of the night," I told the team after doing surveillance. "I'm calling it a night."

"That's not what you used to do," a young guy said.

"I'm not that guy, anymore," I said.

He paused, not in his words, but there was a pause and he didn't drink his own beer down right away.

They see the other side of me now that my timing is dedicated to bigger purposes.

My *unity* had been poisoned with my *Lifestyle of I.mbalance.*

My life was about my career, my friendships, my activities and, even in those areas, I didn't relate to them as something I was doing for the community or my family. It was really about personal glories.

My *intellect* had been poisoned with my *Sense of* **E.ntitlement.**

I had been making bad decisions to keep up good appearances. When I left the metropolitan drug unit after seven years to come into detective work, I was treated as though I was a beginning detective. I had just worked major, multi-agency conspiracy with drug trafficking and wiretaps. I went from that to back to middle-sized, Midwestern town's sheriff's department where I was given mundane cases.

Intellectually, it made sense to move me back into the routine work more slowly, but pride got in way. My ego caused me to have conflict with my bosses, and ultimately direct animosity. I felt like I was being put down and it didn't feel fair. I pushed back and was difficult for others to work with me. When you're in that drug unit environment, you kind of come and go; there's not much structure. At the bureau of detectives, you have a timeline. When I got back to that, they were trying to get me into standard adherence. It was really only going to be three months before I was working more difficult cases. I needed to get back to the roots of investigation and I didn't want to see that purpose.

Identifying the whys behind the need for timing, intellect, and unity was a lesson I hadn't learned early on in my life.

My timing was rededicated to purposeful, meaning connection. I started to go to church and have a relationship with God. I was being led to some of the men's groups in my church and we came together in a positive way, talking about relationships and holding one another accountable. I would have never have done that prior to my transition to faith.

Intellect was all about reading the need for this necessary change in my life; discovering and throwing out the LIE. I needed to win this battle against weight in order to keep winning on life's battlefield.

Unity became targeted toward bringing others together in my life to form unity, and—vital to me during my transformation–accountability. Unity combined togetherness with accountability.

And now?

I also discovered a why that still exists, today. My new purpose was and is serving others. I want to bring people into that unity, help them to intellectually see the transitions they need to take, and identify the timing needed to do so.

On Monday, April 2, 2012, I was at finals week on Extreme Weight Loss. It was the week when the producers and trainers would select who was truly dedicated to move forward with the year-long weight loss transformation.

I called Kelly and told her, "I don't know if I'm gonna make it, but I'm done. I'm in one hundred percent."

It was my Invincible Moment when I had discarded my LIE, aligned my timing, intellect, and unity to an internal why, and ignited on a new journey toward purposefulness.

I told Kelly to get rid of all the alcohol, snacks, processed food, sugar, and on and on I went through a list of the things I knew I shouldn't have around.

"Get some lean proteins, good carbs, and fats, and veggies . . . lots of veggies."

On Monday, April 2nd, I met with the man who would be my off-camera trainer for the next year in Pewaukee, Wisconsin, John Pietenpol. I told him I didn't know if I was going to make the show, but I needed to start.

That was the day – my line in the sand. I was ready to live big . . . but not ugly.

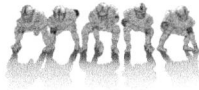

Timing Played A Part . . .

Nine months into my transformation, timing became an important player on my field. I had skin removal surgery to take off eight pounds of excess skin. I was stuck for six weeks without exercise. Being a food addict, what the *Extreme Weight Loss* trainers, Chris and Heidi Powell do, is transition us to exercise addicts. We were working out a minimum of three hours a day. It's as much a part of our lives as brushing our teeth.

I received a note from Chris asking what I was I going to do from here. I utilized those six weeks to journal about each day and, more importantly, about the plans for the rest of my life.

I felt stagnant. I didn't want to be bitter and grumpy at work. As I continue to think about that, I realized that I wanted to be able to share my experience, not just about weight loss, but coaching, policing, faith, and family. The big things . . . and the ugly ones.

I needed to transition from the field of football to the battlefield of life. Regardless of when the struggle occurred, I had something to offer the world. I think I would have gotten to that piece, but the Powell's brought that to me.

Intellect Played A Part . . .

It was important to put a plan in place. I had to tap intentionally into what I needed in order to succeed:

- Meal Preparations
- Routines
    - o Eating five times a day
    - o Exercising seven days a week
- Removal of Temptations
- Knowing My Trigger Foods and Behaviors
- Alcohol
- Pain
- Depression

Intellect means that you have to have Identification and awareness of what you're battling and you must keep away pride and ego as they will prevent such needs. When I was able to identify the barriers preventing me from success, it led into a routine that addressed physical, spiritual, and emotional transformation – something far greater than mere weight loss.

Unity Played A Part . . .

It was important to have positive, good people who could make me think and reflect on your journey. People like that were also important in the beginning of my transformation, simply to help me to identify the need to begin it. As I shared in, *"Live An Extreme Life,"* I even had good friends and colleagues who were willing to hear the hard truths that were hardly wrong:

Toward the end of my stint with the metropolitan drug unit, I had built a good reputation as a reliable drug cop. Sometimes, the work we did would involve the Drug Enforcement Agency (DEA). Their resources were helpful, particularly when we crossed state lines. Our team had been working a bust that was about to go out of our jurisdiction, so this was one of those times when we would have to bring in the federal agencies. We brought the case to them and handled it collaboratively, with the local, state, and federal officers.

I was working with a fellow metropolitan drug unit agent in California; we had been temporarily deputized by the FBI for this case.

The two of us were going to be out on the west coast for a few days and I was taking advantage of the food, the hotel, and the drinks.

We went out that first day and ate like crap, drank too much, and stayed up too late. The next day, it was more junk for breakfast, for lunch, and drinking as early as we could.

By the time it got to dinner that second day, my partner said to me, "Bob, I just can't eat and drink like this. I actually feel sick."

I was embarrassed.
I was hurt.
And I knew he was right.

I wouldn't have been successful if there was a missing unity component during my transition. I needed my trainer. I needed Kelly at home. I needed church to give me strength. I needed my supporters at work. I needed Chris and Heidi Powell. I needed my **Extreme Weight Loss** cast mates. I needed the people who would never be afraid to tell me the hard truths. More than any of the other lessons of my Big Ugly days, unity helped me to stay focused on my external *and* internal whys.

When I walked into my church, I had focus to stay away from temptation. The place of the most temptation and most strength were in same place because my church serves doughnuts. In that community, though, I didn't need them.

At work, most of the guys were complimentary to me. They asked about my experience and it gave me an opportunity to share. It kind of made me feel loved because they wanted to know what was going on in my life. Nobody said a bad word. When there were doughnuts or cookies, they would keep me accountable.

"Bob – you can't have this stuff," they would joke around - a bunch of guys being guys.

Nobody challenged me, though or truly tried to tempt me away from my goal. The integrity I had gained through my faith transformation and my experience with *Extreme Weight Loss* would have made that battle winnable, but I'm glad I didn't have to face it.

When it comes to true unity, too, it doesn't go away when a battle is conquered. If you've built a community on purpose and integrity, they are there for the whole war.

Today, after a lifetime of abusing my own body inside and out, followed by the exertion of getting it back, I am in need of five surgeries on top of the knee replacement I've already had. I'm in pain most days.

I could be mad and sulk or I can take them as they come. "Action conquers fear," as Chris Powell and Dr. Holly talk about. When you have something you're afraid of, the more the fear builds up inside of you; the more it becomes like a consuming cancer. Once you deal with it, you feel better. I'm going to be positive about the upcoming surgeries; it comes back to mental mindset. I can't change my joints. I can't go back and have a redo.

Besides, joints can be repaired, but organs cannot and I've regained a heart that is physically and spiritually healthy. Obesity would have killed me, but a bad shoulder won't.

Even the people I've mentored and been mentored by in the years since my transformation keep me strong. There's Bruce Pitcher, who—despite a horrendous childhood—has chosen to ignite the day, the Invincible Vince Papale, Dr. Holly Wyatt—who has taught me to intertwine purpose with core values on top of the diet and exercise plan, and even local heroes like Chris McIntosh, the Assistant Athletic Director at the University of Wisconsin-Madison. These are the people who cheer me on as I work toward living big, but not ugly, on life's battlefields.

Super Bowl 50's Carolina Panther, Mike Mickens, is a Cornerback out of Cincinnati. He earned All-Big East recognitions for interceptions, pass breakups, and tackles. In his NFL career, Mickens has so far collected 14 picks, 44 pass breakups, 6 interceptions, and an exciting 2 touchdowns off of those interceptions. Despite the outstanding record, one of the number one things that is pointed out about Mickens in his NFL analysis is not his playing, but his coachability and willingness to lead by example.

Are you willing to continue learning like a champion even while already succeeding in transformation like one?

Live Big - Not Ugly!

Chris McIntosh's Five Seconds!

The body follows the mind.

"If you focus on the risks, they'll multiply in your mind and eventually paralyze you. You want to focus on the task, instead, on doing what needs to be done.

~Barry Eisler

A good friend of Bob Brenner's from his law enforcement career was friends with Chris McIntosh and introduced the two of them. Later, the two crossed paths again in Denver when Bob was meeting a new *Extreme Weight Loss* cast. He was living in the Denver area. The two clicked quickly as both were former offensive linemen from Southeast Wisconsin. Chris had gone on after high school to play for the University of Wisconsin – Madison as a Badger and, eventually, the Seattle Seahawks. Chris was an example to Bob of how to do life right, post athleticism. He had always wanted to reach former athletes and here was a guy that, post football career, went from 320 pounds to 240 pounds. He leads an extremely healthy lifestyle and found success after the transition from an athletic life.

Bob met with Chris at a local coffee shop. All 6'7" of Chris walked in looking super lean, well-dressed, and put together. When the two sat down, what impressed Bob immediately was how he talked about family and faith.

In Chris's post-football life, he's used a lot of sporting tactics and applied them to various businesses he started. Today, Bob sees Chris as a good friend and a good mentor. He's positive. He's an example. He understood when he was done playing that he needed to lose weight, exercise, and be healthy. He was active, clean eating, family supportive, and leading a healthy lifestyle. The moral of the story is that, overall, Bob wanted him in his life.

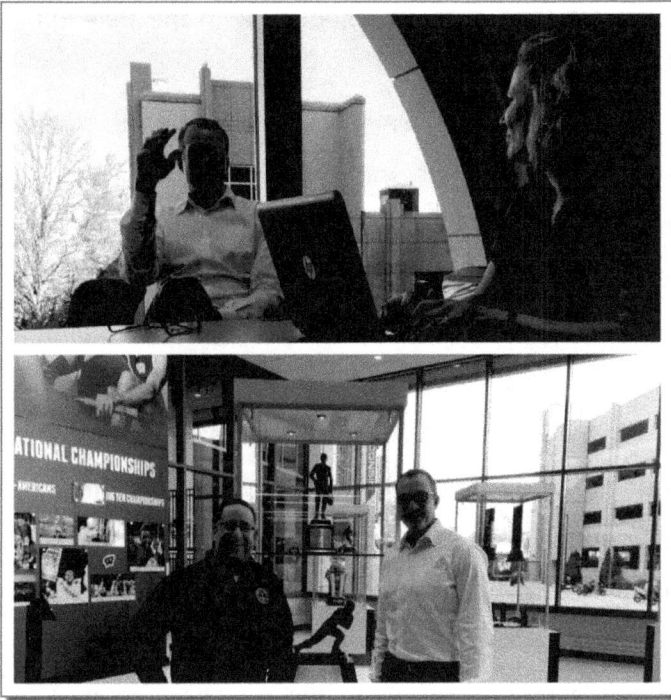

Top: Chris McIntosh interviews for Bob's book.
Bottom: Bob Brenner and Chris McIntosh at UW-Madison.

McIntosh considers himself more of an exception than the rule with regard to his football start. He began in the game relatively late, not playing until he was a freshman at Pewaukee High School. Chris didn't even know the positions of the game when he went to a football camp hosted by Catholic Memorial High School in Waukesha, Wisconsin. What's more is that it turned out he was at the wrong camp; it was for everybody but linemen. McIntosh was a 6'6" tall linebacker. The very next weekend following the camp, he lined up with the Pewaukee High School Pirates.

Four years later, Chris would become the school's first ever athletic scholarship to a Division I School when legendary UW-Madison Coach Bill Calahan showed up with the offer. It wasn't about his playing ability as Chris himself considered himself average, but Calahan saw McIntosh as coachable.

Barry Alvarez and Bill Calahan saw potential in Chris that he didn't see in himself. They did all they could to help him fulfill and achieve that potential. When that happened, it was magical. When it's repeated over and over and over and over again, the result is beautiful.

Chris credits receiving the coaches' support and his getting built by them and experiencing breakthroughs, with how he began to believe that anything is possible. Receiving that support required the coachability that Calahan had honed in on. McIntosh needed the ability to take instruction, regardless of the form or tone of it, and translate it into action or performance.

Every coach had a different style with Chris. His UW line coach, Jim Huber, was very intense. There was a lot of yelling and screaming. He was aware of it and told us to listen to what he say and not how he said it. Chris was able to take that intense barrage and instill it into the key take-aways that would translate into a better performance. As a result, he redshirted as second string as a freshman.

Chris McIntosh's formal University of Wisconsin - Madison Badgers Team Photo

It was a real mind job for Chris to prepare each week to play even though I wouldn't actually be on the field. He leaned about the physical and mental stress of a game, grew an understanding of expectations, and was given exposure to his future teammates

As a starter in his second year, he was a freshman with all seniors on the line. It was overwhelming, but an opportunity.

'Here's my chance. This is why I came here. This is what I want to do,' Chris remembers thinking, but—on other hand—it scared the crap out of him.

Chris worried about how to balance everything. His goal was small: Don't be the guy who screws up. Because he was the kid on the line, when things went wrong, it was usually his fault, whether he deserved it or not.

During that first playing season, McIntosh's confidence hit an all-time-low and it was really frustrating. It went beyond self-confidence. He went through a period of, not just lack of confidence, but lack of self-worth. It's not a good place. Seventy-one out of seventy-two plays, McIntosh would get the job done, but he'd leave thinking about the one play when he failed.

Partway through his season that year, and he never asked who, but *somebody* saw *something* that seemed off and he began to see a sports psychologist. There's not a lot of difference between sports and regular psychologist except for an awareness of athletics. They may understand, to a greater extent, the intricacies of the field players are on.

The focus of Chris's sessions was to create self-awareness. There were certain types of plays in which he wasn't confident. When those plays were called, an automatic reaction was triggered. The psychologist tried to get an understanding of what he went through as a human being, and ultimately recognized that, following a trigger event, (in McIntosh's case, the calling of certain plays), he had maybe five seconds from play call to snap to come up with a way to adapt. He had just five seconds to go from feeling worthless to feeling confident.

If Chris could be purposeful about that fraction of time before a play on the field, he could get past, not just one play, but—through repeated practice—he could adapt to every play. He could face the field (of football *or* life) with confidence.

1 – 2 – 3 – 4 – 5 – GO!

1) AWARENESS:
   - Recognize your own trigger.
   - Acknowledge the fact that you are experiencing a physical, mental, emotional, or other reaction as a result of the trigger.

2) BREATHE:
   - In through your nose.
   - Hold. Get calm.
   - Out through your mouth.

3) TAKE IN THE SCENE:
   - Observe your surroundings.
   - Consider the tangible and the intangible.

4) MENTALLY PREPARE:
   - *Choose* a response.
   - Be intentional

5) PHYSICALLY PREPARE:

- Ask yourself what your choice looks like.
- Make necessary physical adjustments.

GO! STEP OUT IN VULNERABILITY:

- Accept your choice and follow through with your plan.
- Do not consider success or failure at this time.

As a lineman, Chris had five seconds. People often think of "game plans," but in reality, the games we play on sport fields and life's fields are a series of plays. Without a PLAY plan—a plan that allows you to achieve victory at each step—you won't achieve the win in the overall game. By building victory at each step, you are actually building victory for the whole game.

Chris McIntosh's Five Seconds are a play plan that he was able to repeat again and again before each new decision, each new event, and each new challenge. Imagine the power of a play plan for life . . . and, chances are, you have more than a few seconds to figure it out.

In McIntosh's case, his play plan would be implemented for years to come.

Every Friday morning in the winter at Madison, winter conditioning built up the players physically and mentally. Friday mornings at 5:00 the morning was the big test. Everybody went to McClain Field with pits in their stomachs because they didn't know if they were going to make it through the day.

Over the course of five years, Chris became comfortable knowing he'd walk into that environment and, rather than try to save something for the end, he just laid it all out there all the time. The group dynamic was such that it was easier to do it when the guy next to him did it, too. He had some workouts when he had real doubts, but he made it, then he'd an ounce of empowerment and snowball from there . . . a Wisconsin winter snowball ready to plow down the players in front of him.

Chris McIntosh "snowballing" on the field!

Chris was quick to write off the "fall-outs" as people who didn't have it in them and were weak. It's easy to quickly arrive at the conclusion that the team was better off without them. Some didn't have the mental toughness; some recovered and figured out the survival; some didn't.

There are a lot of guys that try to make the High School to Division I transition and don't. Some miss home. Some don't know social campus life. Some come in behind, physically speaking, and have a lot of making up to do. Chris figured out early on who would make it and who wouldn't. (Although later in life, when he couldn't make it any more in Seattle, he saw those "weak fall-outs" in a different light.)

In the year 2000, Chris McIntosh drafted to the Seattle Seahawks under Coach Mike Holmgren. He came in on week one and started in week seven.

Chris McIntosh kept his #75 jersey on his new NFL team.

McIntosh didn't have the same level of confidence in the NFL as he did in college. At the training camp after his first season, he injured his neck and played throughout the season with reduced strength in his left arm. Chris experienced fifty episodes of stingers – a head thrown back with a pinched nerve. He experienced chronic pain, numbness, and loss of strength. McIntosh developed bone spurs in the channels where the nerve comes out.

Despite being a 320 pound lineman who could bench press 500 pounds, he would come home after a game and not be able to hold a gallon of milk. Cortisone injections did nothing. He'd played injured before, but never to the point where he couldn't meet his own or the team's expectations.

McIntosh had surgery before the third season. When he played, he was confident. He played the best he'd ever played for about a week and a half before he took a routine hit . . . and he was out . . . just like that.

Chris had already determined that there was going to be a fork in the road. It wasn't a hard decision to leave Seattle based on the symptoms he was going through.

Chris McIntosh huddles up with the Seahawks.

Chris thought he'd play for a long time. When he says that he knew there was a fork in the road, he didn't really believe it in his heart. He returned to college for a single semester to complete his degree. Then, Chris had his first of three children with Deann, the High School sweetheart who'd married in his rookie year with Seattle. There's a fifty percent rate of divorce within two years of retirement from the NFL. He knew that wasn't the life for him, but he didn't have a clear picture of what he wanted to do. He had enough resources to take a year and a half to think about what the future would be.

He wasn't engaged with work.

He wasn't happy.

You leave professional athletics with patterns:

Perform really well.

Get the job done.

Get back up and do it again.

On the field of life, the cycles were longer and Chris would grow bored, frustrated, or even begin to feel that lack of confidence seep in between plays.

He wasn't transitioning well.

When McIntosh retired from football, he was healthy, but not competing. Deann got into triathlons, but Chris couldn't swim and five knee surgeries meant that he didn't do great on the runs. Because of a love for nature, Chris got into mountains. This was his new goal.

"I couldn't be a 320 lb. man post Seattle," Chris shared. "When the music of football stopped, I weighed 320. I'd been 328 before. I had watched my teammates, when it ended, either go up or down. At 320, the prospect of going up scared me, so I became conscious about it and tried to do something about it."

"I took a look at how I ate and started cooking my own food," he continued. "I began to eat healthy and I lost forty pounds in six months. In fairness, a lot of that was muscle atrophy. The other forty or fifty have been increments that are functions of lifestyle adjustments triathlons didn't work for me, but I like road biking. Then, I started yoga I got into mountaineering. It was a gradual and incremental lifestyle."

"To be honest," he admitted, "I had a lot of frustration with the loss. I wrestle with the fact that I liked being big and strong. Today, I'm not big and I think I'd really like to be stronger than I am. For me, that means more weight training. I kind of wrestle with who I want to be. There are parts of the old Chris McIntosh, the old lineman, that I want to hold onto."

Nutrition and working out helped to lead him from 320 pounds to his post-football career 240 pounds, but he needed something to work toward.

Chris's first mountain-climbing goal was in Mexico. Chris was back with a team, having to show up prepared and when he got there, he got comfortable, again, being uncomfortable. Later, he climbed Denali (formerly known as Mount McKinley) in Alaska. He spent eighteen days on the Mountain enduring some of the toughest physical and mental things he'd ever endured, including an emergency descent.

With competition awakened again in McIntosh, he was able to dare his life forward through practice of the physical and emotional exercises that made him great in football. He's a daily practitioner of meditation. It brings him to center, not just on a mountain top, but in life's moments that require longer cycles. He has somewhere from which to work in moments such as: the birth of all of his children, a job interview, or any time he shows vulnerability by putting forth an idea or leading a charge. These were snap-of-the-ball, vulnerable moments that often would put him back on the line, hearing the trigger call of a play he wasn't sure he could handle.

There was a chance he'd fail. In football, he was going to do it in front of 82,000 people. Then what? That's the piece he had to learn to get right on life's changing fields just as he had done on the football field. The competitive piece gave him things to work for, but the recovery piece includes some form of coping, as well. You may be climbing toward something, but you're walking away from the last play. On a bad day, do you eat more, have an extra glass of wine, disengage, spend the evening on social media, or get too busy?

When we turn to coping mechanisms instead of actually coping, we're forgetting that there's always a next play. The struggle for McIntosh was that he never really got through the worth part of next plays in football.

The reason Chris routinely goes back to "seventy-two" plays is because that's the play he couldn't forget. At UW-Wisconsin, the Badgers played Syracuse in 1997 (against Donovan McNabb). He ran seventy-one of seventy-two plays well. On one play, he took a wrong step and it cost them the touchdown. They got killed in that game and that's the one play he still remembers today.

The inability to let go of the last play was Big Ugly that Chris had to manage in his post-football life.

Out in the world, McIntosh performed really well due to all of the tools that he'd picked up. He still had coachability and winter work ethic (except he kept it all year long). McIntosh went on a scoring streak in real estate and entrepreneurship. He and his family moved to Denver in an excuse to be near mountains. He was killing it on every play.

It wasn't until the inevitable sack occurred, a business that got out of his control which he ultimately had to sell. He never saw it coming. Chris really had to think about how he was wired. Was this life's seventy-second play?

Count to five . . .

1) AWARENESS:
   - Recognize your own trigger.
   - Acknowledge the fact that you are experiencing a physical, mental, emotional, or other reaction as a result of the trigger.

   Chris was triggered by failure.

2) BREATHE:
   - In through your nose.
   - Hold. Get calm.
   - Out through your mouth.

A life breath takes a little longer than a portion of five seconds. Meditate. Get calm.

3) TAKE IN THE SCENE:

- Observe your surroundings.
- Consider the tangible and the intangible.

Just because one business was over didn't mean that McIntosh didn't have options.

4) MENTALLY PREPARE:

- *Choose a response.*
- Be intentional

Chris needed a plan to move forward. In Thanksgiving of 2014, he got inducted into UW Madison's Hall of Fame. It was a great experience for his whole family. The school's beloved Barry Alvarez and McIntosh caught up. When he returned to Denver, he sent a thank you note and told him about the positive impact the time had on his family. Barry responded by asking Chris to call him back to consider making an Athletic Director position his next project . . . his seventy-third play.

5) PHYSICALLY PREPARE:

- Ask yourself what your choice looks like.
- Make necessary physical adjustments.

Chris returned to the place that contributed to who he became and he took his fifteen years of experiences on and off the fields back to where it all began. It was a cool opportunity and an awesome place to be.

GO! STEP OUT IN VULNERABILITY:

- Accept your choice and follow through with your plan.
- Do not consider success or failure at this time.

Today, McIntosh's goal is to make an impact. He believes that, because of his experience as a student athlete, it impacts lives. It's not just winning games, it's the Friday mornings, the sports psychology; it's the vulnerability and the academics. Those things make a difference.

Scan here to learn about McIntosh's role at UW-Madison.
http://uwbadgers.com/sportfile.aspx?filename=chris-McIntosh-associate-athletic-director-for-business-development&file_date=2/4/2016#

He speaks to the team and the alumni and asks them, "What did it mean to you? Would you be the same person without it?" So far, he hasn't met somebody who doesn't have that answer, recognizing how sports have changed their lives. He can get passionate about that. He believes in that. To be able to impact the experience, and try to communicate to the staff the WHY of what happens on the fields of play is a big deal. It's the idea that we're not in the business of winning games; we're in the business of elevating the lives of 850 kids who are the athletic students of our school, every year, to bring purpose to all of them.

"I miss the camaraderie of the game," McIntosh said. "There was a lot of downtime in travel and sitting around and B.S.-ing, and telling jokes, and a lot of characters in the locker room, and the stories of what's going on in their lives . . . I miss that the most. I miss competing. I sometimes watch our team. I don't miss feeling like I've been hit by a car for months," Chris ruminates.

It's a constant, never-ending, purposeful effort by Chris, to make family and his new career into his camaraderie, again. It's a balancing act. The play right now is about how to apply awareness and engagement on the new field because the most important play is not the seventy-second one. It's the one we're running right now in the moment. It's number seventy-three. If you want to live big but not ugly, you need to bring it back to the huddle, let go of seventy-two, and get on to the next one, stepping out in vulnerability.

Only 6.5% of high school football players go on to play at the college level. Of those, only 1.6% of players are drafted by the NFL. In other words, out of 1.1 million players at the youth level, a mere 1.1 thousand can expect to "go pro."

There is life after football . . . and after any kind of glory day. What are you going to do for the rest of your life of glory?

5

My big life is not about me.

"There are no coincidences in life. What person that wandered in and out of your life was there for some purpose, even if they caused you harm. Sometimes, it doesn't make sense the short periods of time we get with people, or the outcomes from their choices. However, if you turn it over to God he promises that you will see the big picture in the hereafter. Nothing is too small to be a mistake."

~Shannon L. Alder

When you go through a transformation, there's a tendency to hear the GPS voice in your head saying, "You have arrived." We make it through our own transitions and believe our journeys are done, as if our lives are disconnected from those we touch. We believe we get to simply coast out the rest of our lives at the destination. It may sound like a reasonable or expected goal, but—in reality—human nature doesn't allow endings, only new beginnings.

What if "one small step for man; one giant leap for mankind" was a destination instead of a journey. It would have meant that decades of space exploration that followed wouldn't have occurred. That time in space has led to everything from treatments for ailments to household products that are staples in our lives. Look back even further. What if an unmanned launch left the "you have arrived" message, then that giant leap would never have occurred. Heck, what if you went all the way back to the Wright brothers, to twelve-second flights over Kitty Hawk, North Carolina? If that were the voice calling, "you have arrived," what would our world look like, today?

You could go back to just about any timeline of human history and you'll find countless men and women who could have arrived, but—thank God for the rest of us— chose to stay on the journey. History is made up of people who were always looking for the next play. They didn't settle on glory days, but went on, instead, to create lives of glory, We may not all be given the ability to plant a flag on a low-gravity playing field, but we all have the power to take flight on the purposes in our own lives.

For a long time in my life, I treated football as my "you have arrived" moment. Even when I was in police work, my coaching of football took precedent over many of my life's priorities. It was a BIG, UGLY, LIE. I didn't need a destination moment; I needed an invincible one to take me from the playing fields to the next plays on life's battlefields: my relationships, my home, my career, my finances, my church, and my purpose.

Few moments in my life have felt like destinations as much as the conclusion of my *Extreme Weight Loss* transformation:

> *Stepping onto the scale . . . just a regular scale, not a commercial one . . . no matter what the number was, I knew I'd made it. The number didn't hurt to confirm it, though . . . I was calm. I was at peace finally comfortable in my skin and right where I was supposed to be. The scale stopped chirping at 195 lbs. I had lost over 250 pounds in 365 days! 56% of my bodyweight had fallen off, yet I never felt fuller! I felt like I was on top of the world that day and I've felt like that ever since.*

It wasn't an ending. It was a new beginning.

Bob with his family from left to right, Jordan, Bob, Kelly, and Kayla.

In my new beginning, I learned how to bring my lessons of **Timing**, **Intellect**, and **Unity** on a journey that was bigger than my biggest me to accomplish all of the plays before me: relationships, finances, church, career, home and purpose. I married the concept of Dr. Holly's **Internal Why** to my Big Ugly lessons, used those tools to take advantage of **Invincible Moments**, on which I would **Ignite**, and—if I ever hesitated, I simply **Took Five** before **Stepping Out in Vulnerability**.

My life became big, but my big life is not about me.

Bob laughs with "his old self" at a speaking event in 2015.

It's not even about the incredible people I met *after* I had "arrived."

It's about helping others who are struggling with the challenges of transitioning from playing fields to the ever-changing fields of life.

It's about taking flight, far beyond the glory days and into a life of glory.

It's about finding victory after our seventy-second plays and never arriving until the game clock of life has ticked its last tock.

That's how you live big . . . but not ugly.

References

"12 Most Embarrassing Premature Celebrations in Sports
History." *Last Angry Fan RSS.*, 21 Aug. 2013. Web.
8 Jan. 2016.

"The 3 Stances of Offensive Linemen." *ACTIVE.com.* Web.
8 Jan. 2016.

"The Best Trick Plays in NFL History." *NFL.com.* Web. 8
Jan. 2016.

Brenner, Bob, Reji Laberje, and Chris Powell. *Live an
Extreme Life!: Losing the Weight and Gaining My
Purpose.* Print.

"Bruce Pitcher." Personal interview. Oct. 2015.

"Chris McIntosh." Personal interview. Oct. 2015.

"The Coin Toss: What Could Go Wrong? | Football
Zebras." *Football Zebras.* Web. 8 Jan. 2016.

"Destination Boot Camp - Anschutz Center." *Anschutz
Health and Wellness Center Extreme Weight Loss*

Destination Boot Camp Comments. Web. 8 Jan. 2016.

"Dr. Holly Wyatt." Telephone interview. 13 Jan. 2016.

ESPN. ESPN Internet Ventures, Web. 8 Jan. 2016.

"Extreme Weight Loss TV Show - ABC.com." *ABC*. Web. 8 Jan. 2016.

"Football Trivia And Facts!" *Football Trivia And Facts RSS*., Web. 8 Jan. 2016.

"Football Trivia And Facts!" *Football Trivia And Facts RSS*., Web. 8 Jan. 2016.

Hill, James O., Holly Wyatt, and Christie Aschwanden. *State of Slim: Fix Your Metabolism and Drop 20 Pounds in 8 Weeks on the Colorado Diet*. Print.

"History of Flight." *History of Flight*. Web. 8 Jan. 2016.

IMDb. IMDb.com, Web. 8 Jan. 2016.

"Keith Jackson." *Wikipedia*. Wikimedia Foundation, Web. 8 Jan. 2016.

"Lineman (gridiron Football)." - *Wikipedia, the Free Encyclopedia*. Web. 8 Jan. 2016.

Lucado, Max, Max Lucado, and Max Lucado. *In the Eye of the Storm: The Applause of Heaven*. Nashville, TN: Thomas Nelson, 1999. Print.

"NFL Events: Combine Player Profiles - Mike Mickens." *NFL Events: Combine Player Profiles - Mike Mickens*. Web. 8 Jan. 2016.

"The O-line: Are Football's Big Uglies Ready?" *Scout.com*. Web. 8 Jan. 2016.

Papale, Vince, and Chad Millman. *Invincible: My Journey from Fan to NFL Team Captain*. New York: Hyperion, 2006. Print.

Papale, Vince, Janet Cantwell-Papale, and Tim Vandehey. *Be Invincible!: A Playbook for Reaching Your Full Potential*. Cherry Hill, NJ: Vince Papale Promotions, 2011. Print.

"Pat Tillman Foundation | Investing in Military Veterans
and Their Spouses through Educational
Scholarships." *Pat Tillman Foundation Home
Comments*. Web. 8 Jan. 2016.

"Quotes About Inspirational Success Failure." *(193
Quotes)*. Web. 8 Jan. 2016.

Roth, JD, prod. "Extreme Weight Loss Season 3 Episode
13." *Extreme Weight Loss*. ABC. 03 Sept. 2013.
Television.

Roth, JD, prod. "Extreme Weight Loss Season 4 Episode
4." *Extreme Weight Loss*. ABC. 24 June 2014.
Television.

"Seahawks.com Blog | April Madness: Alexander vs.
Trufant." *Seahawkscom Blog RSS*. Web. 8 Jan.
2016.

"Utah Man Confronts His Abusive Father on 'Extreme
Weight Loss'" *The Salt Lake Tribune*. Web. 8 Jan.
2016.

"Vince Papale." Telephone interview. 29 Dec. 2015.

"WHERE ARE THEY NOW? The First-round Picks from

    Tom Brady's Infamous 2000 NFL Draft - Business

    Insider." *Business Insider*. 02 Oct. 2015. Web. 8

    Jan. 2016.

Index of QR Codes

Electronic Resource Hub
"The Big Uglies"
www.rejilaberje.com/bo
b-brenner.html

Scan here to learn more
about **"Destination Boot
Camp"**
http://anschutzwellness
.com/weight-
loss/extreme-weight-
loss-destination-boot-
camp/

Scan here to purchase
"Live An Extreme Life"
http://www.amazon.co
m/Live-Extreme-Life-
Gaining-
Purpose/dp/09893095
84/ref=asap_bc?ie=UTF
8

Scan here to purchase
Invincible Books
http://www.vincepapale
.com/invinciblebooks.ht
ml

Scan here to get a glimpse into Bob's speaking career.

https://youtu.be/dzFJLrQ_yYU

Scan here to purchase **"State of Slim"**

http://www.stateofslim.com/

Scan here to learn about McIntosh's role at UW-Madison.

http://uwbadgers.com/sportfile.aspx?filename=chris-McIntosh-associate-athletic-director-for-business-development&file_date=2/4/2016#

Index of Photos

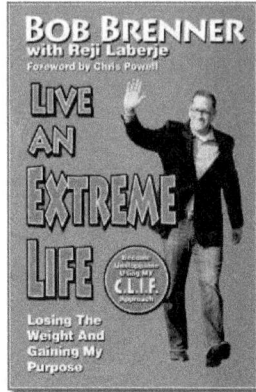

"Live An Extreme Life" - Page 7

Book signing - Page 13

Bob's police retirement - Page 14

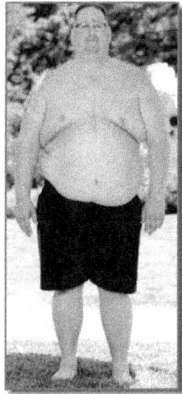

Bob's Pre-weight loss obesity – Page 42

Bruce Pitcher - Page 47

Bruce and Bob with their significant others - Page 49

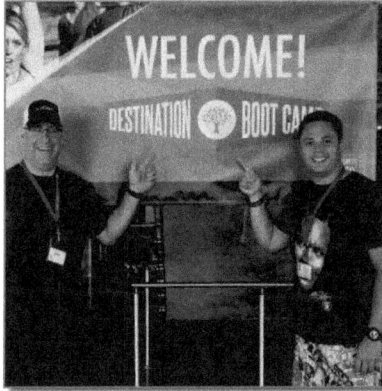

Bruce and Bob at Destination Boot Camp - Page 52

Coach Bruce - Page 57

Bruce's first love, food - Page 61

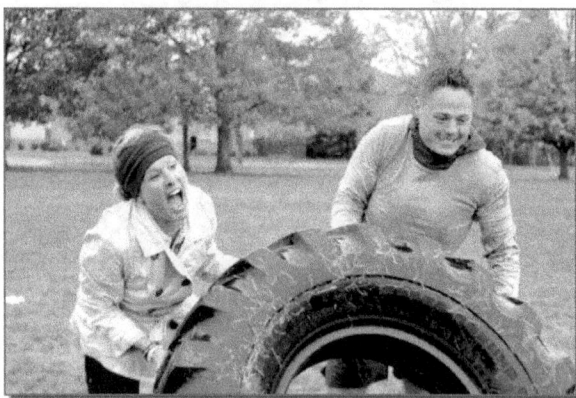

Bruce at Destination Boot Camp - Page 63

Bruce before and after weight loss - Page 67

Bruce and Bob strike a pose - Page 68

Bruce and fiancée, Alexa - Page 69

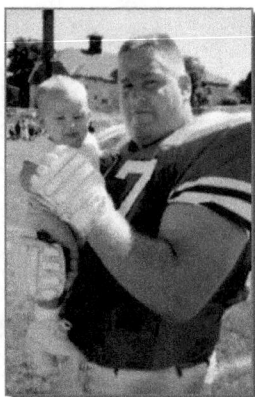

Bob and his daughter Kayla - Page 76

Vince Papale today - Page 86

Philadelphia Eagle Vince Papale - Page 92

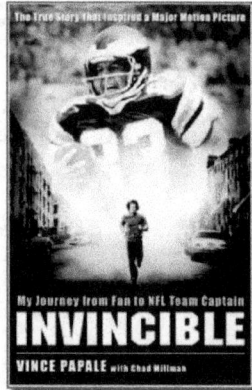

Papale's first book, "Invincible" - Page 97

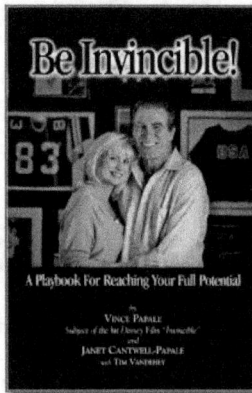

Papale's second book, "Be Invincible - Page 99

Dr. Holly Wyatt - Page 115

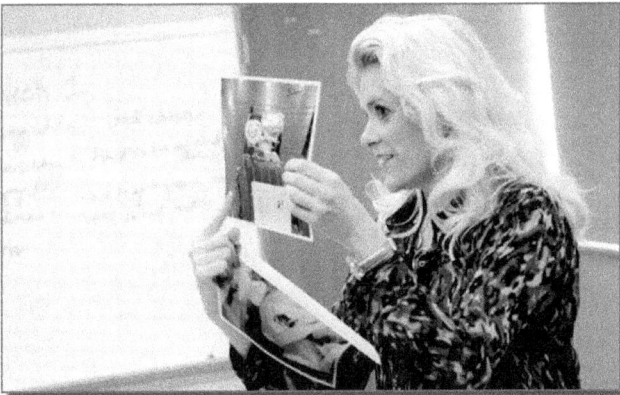

Dr. Holly at Destination Boot Camp - Page 119

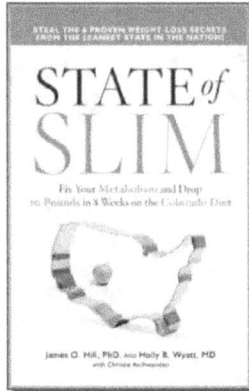

Dr. Holly's Book, "State of Slim" - Page 124

Chris McIntosh with UW-Madison today - Page 149

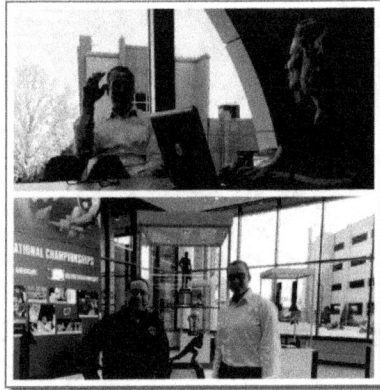

Chris interviews for Bob's book - Page 151

McIntosh as a redshirt Freshman - Page 154

McIntosh stands his ground - Page 160

Draft day - Page 161

McIntosh with the Seahawks - Page 163

Bob with his family - Page 178

Bob then and now - Page 179

Acknowledgments

I'd like to offer my sincere thanks to all of those who helped to bring this project together including, but not limited to, the writing, editing, publishing and marketing teams of Reji Laberje Author Programs, and contributors: Chris McIntosh, Vince Papale, Bruce Pitcher, and Dr. Holly Wyatt.

I also remain grateful for the staffs, crews, and participants of Extreme Weight Loss, Destination Boot Camp, and Anschutz Health and Wellness Center.

Thank you to the friends, families, and colleagues of those whose stories are represented in these pages.

Last, but never least, I give thanks and gratitude to Jesus Christ, my savior and the reason living big is possible for any of us.

~Bob

Co-Authors (And Good Friends) Bob & Reji
Bond Over The Release Of Their Second Joint Title

After decades in the football world as a player, and later as a coach, as well as working primarily in the narcotics unit with the Waukesha County (Wisconsin) Sheriff's Department, Bob Brenner found himself breaking the scales at 448 pounds. From 2012 to 2013, he dropped 56% of that bodyweight following a faith transformation documented in his first book, *"Live An Extreme Life."* He kept the weight off and the transformation led to a successful career as a motivational coach and speaker. Today, Bob lives in Fort Collins, Colorado with his wife of more than twenty years, Kelly.

Working with Bob to create his book was author, Reji Laberje, of Reji Laberje Author Programs, LLC., where their vision is to use meaningful writing to, for, and from you to make far-reaching, positive impacts. Learn more at www.rejilaberje.com.